A Prostitute's
Guide to Success

A Prostitute's Guide to Success

My Life, Struggles and Successes

Tanisha Nicole Billops

Brilliant Minds
Publications, llc

Brilliant Minds Publications, LLC
Copyright © 2016 Tanisha Nicole Billops
All rights reserved.

ISBN: 0692773002
ISBN 13: 9780692773000

"The best way to predict your future is to create it."
- *Abraham Lincoln*

Dedication

To my precious children, Cameron and Iyonna: I wish I could give you the life of your dreams, but so far I've only given you life. It is now your responsibility to create your dreams. Be all you can be and more! I wrote this book for you, so that you know where you come from. Like this book, I hope your life is filled with many meaningful chapters.

This book is also dedicated to my friends, family, and teachers who have encouraged me to keep trying, even when I didn't have the focus or desire to do so.

Lastly, this book is dedicated to girls and boys, young or old. Be willing to do anything that it takes to find happiness! It doesn't matter how rich or poor we may be, we all deserve happiness and deserve to live life to the fullest. Remember, we cannot judge the value of our lives by the neighborhood we grew up in, or the accumulation of life's things, or what others perceive us to be. Even if we feel broken and confused, there is hope. There are infinite possibilities even if the situation seems hopeless. We live in a great, beautiful, and fulfilling Universe that can deliver to us anything our hearts desire. There's great potential for all our lives; we simply have to be willing to dream a little bit more, worry a bit less, and truly feel and trust in a higher power to make things work out. Anything is possible.

Table of Contents

Prologue

This book was in my head for many years before I wrote it. I had some reservations about writing a story based on my life and experiences. I mentioned the names of people who have made a lasting impact on my life. I thought about what others would think, and how this novel would impact the people I mention in it. My intentions aren't to throw anyone under the bus. I intend no harm to the individuals that I name in this memoir. I've been faithful to my memory, but of course my subjects may remember things differently.

It took some time to get my thoughts out and on paper. I first started writing about my life almost six years before being published. When I finally did, a waterfall of emotions came pouring out. With that, came the difficulty of sorting through all of the emotional baggage that came tied to certain memories. It wasn't until I started reflecting, and taking this writing thing seriously, that I realized that some of the negative emotions I still carried with me were affecting my day-to-day actions, moods, and experiences.

I was the type of person who moved forward from painful experiences with pride, trying to continue on with everyday life. That's what we have to do…right? Without really reflecting on what had happened. But, behind closed doors, it was a different story. I was angry, moody, and depressed. This was because I had never really dealt with or even acknowledged my emotions and where they came from.

Writing this book was a bittersweet experience. Writing about my thoughts and experiences was sometimes a challenge. I felt kind of like a tape recorder after hitting the rewind button. I had to rewind and bring back many almost forgotten memories; some of them good, and others... well, not so much.

At one point, I tried to talk myself out of publishing my story. I was in the midst of some life turmoil. I knew I wanted things to be different in my life, but I was scared to change and stuck in a reality that I didn't want. I had hope that someday things would be different, and that I would gain a new perspective from my experiences. Sometimes, only hope can get us out of a rut. At the time, I made some bad decisions and had to live with the results. The pleasant, and even unpleasant, experiences of my life compelled me to tell my story.

First, I had to overcome my fears about telling my story. I dreamt too much before and had failed at it. I was a mother of two children—a black, single mother at that. I wasn't a famous athlete or movie star. I had never written or published a book. *Who would want to read it?* I thought to myself. You know, the usual thoughts that pop up when you are trying to talk yourself out of a crazy idea. So, I came up with excuses to smother my desire to be a writer.

My life has been an amazing roller coaster of ups and downs, and even with some loop-da-loops from time to time. I've played various roles: mother, employee, wife, and friend. Once, I had dreams of pursuing modeling and acting. I've owned and operated my own businesses—some successful and others failures before they even got started. I've experienced being poor and on welfare, and have also experienced wealth. I've experienced adversity as an African American woman living in the United States. I've felt joy, abundance, pain, heart break, despair, and hundreds of other emotions. I've witnessed firsthand bigotry and racism. I've even battled major depression. Without judgment, I looked back at my trials and tribulations—now being able to see the bigger picture.

For years, fear and depression had me in their grip. I learned to pick myself up after being bankrupt both financially and spiritually. At one time, I was in a depressive cycle. Negative thoughts led to negative emotions, thus creating negative consequences and results—living a habitual pattern for years. It became a cycle that I became too familiar with for nearly a decade, and it took me over six years to finally get out of it. What I learned from negative experiences is that, whatever doesn't kill you will only make you stronger. Through experience and research, I've learned that the mind has greater potential than we know. If you focus on something long enough, whether it is good or bad, the results will manifest, good or bad. If you choose to focus on negativity, negativity will follow. If you choose to focus on happiness, happiness will come into your life. It just depends on what we choose to focus our minds, time, and energy on.

Considering that I'm now an optimist—a person who tries to look at the brighter side of things—even when things aren't going as planned, I do not view negative experiences as such a bad thing. Sometimes struggle is necessary for growth. Surely, when we're living through some of our worst experiences, we don't always perceive it that way; but, when the storm finally clears, we will see the horizon.

Writing this book may not have been an action that I would have taken if I hadn't lived the contrast that inspired me to tell my story. Many of what I considered to be "negative" life experiences at the time—seeing them as awful—I look back at them now with a non-judgmental eye. They were actually blessings in disguise. Many of us don't know how smart we've become from our experiences. I've come to realize that experience is the best teacher! I will discuss life changing experiences, and the obstacles I've overcome. I include in depth details about said experiences, good and bad.

Relationships have played a significant role in my life. There have been many incredible people who have come into my life to serve a great purpose in helping me find my personal success. As I started to write, I couldn't help but focus on intimate relationships and how these relationships have shaped who I am today. Undeniably, the relationships I've had with others have helped me learn more about life and myself in general.

In this book, I bring up prostitution. The sad reality is that for many women it's the only means of income. A black girl in the United States has a better chance of becoming a prostitute than a doctor. It is one of the world's oldest professions, but still a very taboo topic. Many studies of prostitution are biased as well as sexist. While these studies examine the behaviors of the women, they exclude the behaviors or psychology of the men who buy them. My goal is to pull the lid off the sex industry and expose it. Though it is underground, prostitution is one of America's largest and most profitable industries. Prostitution in the United States is a 14.5 billion dollar-a-year business. According to the Urban Institute, there is more cash flowing through the sex industry than drugs and guns combined in many American cities.

Furthermore, the general textbook definition of prostitution is: a man or woman who willingly uses his or her talent or ability in a base and unworthy way, usually for money. There have been many times when I have worked using my talents for money, sometimes in a base or unworthy way. I worked, even though I didn't feel as if I were getting enough in return for the effort I was putting forth. I worked hard, sometimes pouring my passions into something only to see little or no return. There were times when the energy and effort that I put into others was not always given back to me. Many of us continue day in and day out, putting forth ALL our energy for little or nothing in return. While our conscience screams out in the form of stress, bitterness, depression, anxiety, and a plethora of other emotions. We hope for something better—or maybe we don't even expect anything in return.

I wrote this book to tell my story. After some pain, heartbreak, trials, and tribulations, I have learned to live a happy life. I have learned from my experiences. I have changed the way I think about things to bring lasting, positive changes into my life. I discuss my struggles, but most importantly, how I overcame them. My journey has changed my outlook completely. The only way I was finally able to remove my wall of emotional baggage was to move on from my habitual negative thinking patterns.

I put my attention toward truly moving on from the effects of the baggage. You will see how I attempted to make the most out of my traumatic experiences by reflecting back and learning. To me, success is when you go through life-changing events only to lose yourself, then encounter a turning point, and you find yourself all over again. Hopefully, the example of my life will help others live their meaning of success.

Chapter 1

Know Thy Self

I sat up on the plush pillow-top mattress. I wore a long, white, flowing summer dress. My hair was straight and pulled back into a loose, messy ponytail. Mascara ran down my cheeks like black tears. I was worn out with life. I fantasized about pressing a cold, hard steel barrel against the temple of my head and pulling the trigger. Many questions raced through my mind like a bullet train as I thought about ending it all. Would I leave a note for my family? If not, they would wonder what I thinking and why I took such drastic measures. I started to think about how my son would continue living without a mother. *He's such a good boy*, I thought to myself. If I ended my life, he would end up being a cold, heartless person who felt as though his mother had abandoned him when he needed her the most. I started to feel sick inside.

My daughter was still a baby, so she wouldn't remember me much. *If I wasn't here, who would take care of her and teach her about being a woman?* I didn't want to think about it. Just the thought of being away from my children made my stomach turn into a knot. I wouldn't allow them to go through life knowing that their mother took hers. The tears brought too much pain to comprehend.

I sat the pistol back onto the top shelf of the closet. "I'm going crazy," I said quietly to myself. Even if I was going crazy, I couldn't give into to it. I tried to erase the thought. Sometimes the stress and unhappiness seemed too much. At the end of the day, I knew I had to keep going. If not for me, for my children.

Just a few months prior, things were going well. I was on my way to becoming a millionaire—at least, that's what I told myself.

Three years prior, I just had gotten married. We lived in a million-dollar home, drove a hundred-thousand-dollar car, and had a thriving real estate business that I started from scratch. It seemed like almost overnight, everything went from perfect to disaster. To completely understand my story, one must understand where I've come from—where it all began.

I grew up in a place they call the Silicon Valley. It's nicknamed for the southern portion of the San Francisco Bay area in northern California. The name "Silicon Valley" eventually came to refer to all of the high-tech businesses in the area. Most people are familiar with technology empires like eBay, Yahoo, Google, and Tesla. All of these companies started in the Silicon Valley. Well known entrepreneurs, like Steve Jobs, worked out of his garage.

I grew up specifically in San Jose, which is in the center of Silicon Valley. San Jose is unlike any other large city in the world. San Jose is a coastal city, not too far away from the ocean. It's only thirty minutes away from San Francisco, and with its bustling freeway system, it connects multiple cities together though out the Bay Area. San Jose is also known as one of America's richest and poorest cities. That's because the disparity between wealth is vast. In 2014, the median income was just about $100,000. In the twenty-five years preceding the middle of 2001, San Jose housing prices had grown by 936 percent. This is more than any other major urban area in the world.

San Jose nearly quintupled in population from 1950 through 1970, representing an incredible 8 percent annual growth rate. By comparison, Las Vegas—the fastest growing major U.S. city in the last decade—is growing at only about 6 percent per year. Part of San Jose's growth was due to an aggressive annexation program. Annexation is the process by which cities extend their municipal services, regulations, voting privileges, and taxing authority to new territory. Many African Americans migrated to cheaper areas out of the Bay Area in the late 1990's, deeming San Jose too expensive to afford to live comfortably. Today, African Americans account for just around 3.5 percent of the population in the city of San Jose.

In the 1960's and 1970's, both my maternal and paternal grandparents chose to raise their children in the Bay Area. My grandparents chose to live in San Jose for many reasons: San Jose was a good place to live, crime was low, the weather was nice and temperate, homes were cheap, and jobs were plentiful. Revolutionary companies like Google and Facebook hadn't made their mark on public perception yet. When they moved to the Silicon Valley, San Jose was a quiet suburban city. Then, the microprocessor was invented. And now, hardly anyone can imagine life without personal technology.

I'm starting my story from the time San Jose was full of orchards, fruit trees, farms, and cheap land. San Jose is one of the largest valley's in California, but I'm clearly not your typical valley girl. My birth marked a bittersweet moment for my family. I was raised by an extended family. When I was born, my parents were just teenagers. My mother and father dated in high school and became each other's first "experience." Both of my parents came from middle class African American families. My mom, Lisa, is the middle child of five. Jerome, my father, was the only boy out of four children.

My mom's parents, Billy and Vernita, were very involved in my up-bringing. Grandpa Billy felt that Jerome was sneaky and couldn't be trusted; it was just more of a feeling than anything. Grandpa Billy was known for being a good judge of character. There was just something about Jerome that he didn't like. He disliked him from day one; he called him a, "snake in the grass." Grandpa Billy often used expressions to describe people, especially people he disliked. Grandpa Billy didn't have much family growing up. So, he made sure that his family now was always close. He grew up with just his mother. With dark skin, average height, and a solid build, he always got complimented on his nice, white teeth and pink gums. He had a dimpled smile that invited others in. Grandpa Billy always stayed clean cut. As a child, his mother was a hairdresser. She styled, maintained, and cut for white people, as well as black people. His mom used to tell him, "White folks already look down on blacks, so you must look your best boy, at all times. So they won't see a reason to look down on you!"

Before Grandpa Billy laid eyes on my Nana, he had never seen a girl so beautiful. She had a honey brown complexion, large almond shaped brown eyes, and in the sun, Grandpa noticed that Nana's long thick hair had a golden brown hue to it. One day, while he waited for Nana like always—he stood on the corner across from her school; far away enough to not be noticed, but close enough to have a view of her when she came out of the brick building—Grandpa Billy saw two white boys approach her and say something.

Grandpa noticed her face change from happy complacency, into a nervous frown. Nana was one of the only black students who attended her school. Sometimes, people were rude or picked on her. Because she didn't say anything back to the boys, they just laughed and walked off before Grandpa could get across the street to come to her aide. That day, he introduced himself, and after that Grandpa Billy walked Nana home from school every day.

Nana loved school and did very well. She was at the top of her class. Grandpa Billy liked that she was smart. As they walked on the dirt road to her house in Fresno, she recited what she had learned that day. "Since you go to school with all them white folks, I knew you had to be smart," Grandpa said. Nana giggled. Billy had a great sense of humor and always made Nana laugh.

Grandpa himself had never really gone to school. When he did, they didn't teach him much, or he was getting in trouble. He figured he was better at hustling and making money than going to school. Where he was from, schools hadn't integrated yet. He was from Beaumont, Texas, a small town on the Louisiana and Texas border. Grandpa and his mom had recently moved to Fresno. He didn't know how to read, but Grandpa Billy managed just as well as the next person who could. Besides, he was better with numbers. Although he lacked formal education, he was very intelligent. He enjoyed talking to people and could hold a conversation with the best of them. He held himself with dignity and expected to be respected.

Nana's mother was weary of Grandpa Billy at first. She knew that he wanted to marry Nana—he had told her so. Nana and her mother were close and she didn't want to see her daughter go. Nana's mother was a dark-skinned woman with long hair that, over the years, had greyed prematurely. She was stern, but very loving. She just wanted the best for her child. Nana had a father who was part German. He was tall, slim, and fair-skinned with light green eyes. He worked in the coalmines in Arizona. His lungs couldn't tolerate the smoke, and he died from lung cancer in his forties. After that, Nana's family relocated to Fresno for better job prospects. There was plenty of work in the fields. Nana was the third child of four. In the summer, she picked cotton with her brother and sisters to earn money.

Growing up as a black person in the 1950's, there weren't too many options. It was 1950 and US President Truman ordered ground troops into action. Nana graduated from high school, and shortly after, Grandpa Billy was drafted into the United States Military. He was going to be stationed in Monterey, California. Before he left, he asked for Nana's hand in marriage, and she accepted his proposal.

The Cold War had begun. Grandpa Billy and Nana lived in an apartment on base. The Cold War was the first armed conflict in the global struggle between democracy and communism. They both knew that the government was shipping troops overseas to fight in combat. One evening, Grandpa Billy came home from work at the base. His face was sad. He plopped down and said in a solemn tone, "It was just a matter of time." He would be shipped away to war in Korea.

Nana found out she was pregnant with their first child. A black lady worked in the administrative office at the base. During a conversation, Grandpa Billy had mentioned to her that he was an only child. She said, "If you are your mother's sole-surviving son, and you can prove it, you could get an honorary discharge." The US military has Special Separation Policies. He was able to bring in documentation showing that he was his mother's only surviving son and wasn't shipped to Korea after all.

After Grandpa was discharged from the military, Nana gave birth to their first child. They named her Vanessa and moved to Berkley, California. Nana got a job as a Switchboard Operator while Grandpa stayed home with the baby. This was very unconventional at that time, but it was easier for Nana to find work than it was for Grandpa Billy. When Nana got paid, she gave the check to her husband. When she got off work, he expected her to have his bath water drawn and dinner ready when he got out of the bath. At that time, he was just being a typical southern man. Nana kept up with the demands because, like a typical wife in the 1960's, she wanted to keep her husband happy. She eventually stopped working as a Switch Operator once she discovered she was pregnant with their second child—named Keith.

As I mentioned before, Grandpa Billy was better at hustling and numbers than anything else. In the evenings, he got dressed up. Leaving his wife and kids at home, he went out to the Oaks Club, one of the oldest poker card clubs in Northern California. At the club, they had live jazz bands playing music, booze, and gambling. Grandpa loved jazz music. The smooth sound of the saxophone with its melodic tone and the light background drumming was hypnotic and relaxing. Grandpa Billy's drink of choice was Vodka and orange juice. At the club, he was well liked and respected. When he went, he made an appearance. He'd make sure he had a fresh haircut and that his shoes were shined. He dressed up in a suite, derby hat, and trench coat—looking sharp as always.

Many times, when Grandpa went out, he didn't come home from the club until the next morning—at the break of dawn, smelling of cigarettes and Vodka. This irritated Nana, but she thought it was best to not ask any questions; especially because when he came home, he came home with wads of cash. Gambling was one thing that Grandpa Billy was good at. So, Nana didn't question him about his whereabouts. She kept it to herself and tried to focus on their children. Nana was a good mother. Sometimes, she had a habit of putting others' needs before her own, but that was the kind of person she was. Naturally, she was a very patient, nurturing, and caring person.

By 1962, Nana was pregnant for the third time. The Walker family was starting to outgrow their small two-bedroom home in Berkley. Grandpa Billy met a gentleman at the card club and was offered a job at a new General Motors plant they had just opened in Fremont. My grandparents had saved some money—enough to buy a new home.

Another one of Grandpa's friends from the card room suggested that he take a look in San Jose. "There's lots of land and new homes in San Jose going for cheap!" his friend told him. Grandpa took his advice and drove the family out to San Jose. That same day, they found a modest three-bedroom home in their price range in San Jose's east side. The new home was bigger than their home in Berkley. The home was located in a neighborhood near a high school called Mt. Pleasant. It was in a multicultural neighborhood made up of blacks, Hispanics, and a few white families living out, what they considered then, to be the American dream. My grandparents paid $9,000 cash for the single story home. That was considered big money at the time, especially since banks wouldn't lend to blacks.

With their move to San Jose, Nana continued to be a housewife and full-time mother. She still hated when Billy was gone. When he wasn't at work, he went to the card room. Sometimes, he was gone for days at a time. Smoking cigarettes and shopping helped to ease her nerves. She also read a lot of books; she enjoyed reading romance novels. Reading helped Nana relax. Before bedtime, she read her romance novel so that she could get lost in another world.

The family lived comfortably. Grandpa took time off to take his family on road trips and vacations. My grandparents had a total five children. Out of three girls and two boys, Lisa (my mother) was the middle child. Nana considered my mom the best behaved out of all five of her children. With her bubbly personality and easy going attitude, Mom was the peacemaker and people pleaser of the family. She was smart, free spirited, and maintained good grades. She listened well in school and did what she was told.

After not coming home one night, Grandpa Billy came strolling in through the front door early the next morning. Nana was already up, sitting on the couch—lit cigarette in hand waiting for him. She hadn't gotten any sleep the night before. On her beige face, deep brown bags hung under her large almond-shaped eyes. Him coming home late at night, and sometimes not even at all, was taking a toll on her. Nana and my mom had a unique bond; she knew when her mother was upset. During those times, my mom helped Nana clean and cook for the family.

As the middle child, Mom got away with a lot of things that her other siblings didn't. She was a bit sneaky and didn't let her parents know about the boy she was dating. My mom had brown skin, a petite frame, and wore glasses. While Nana's mind was occupied, Mom took full advantage of the opportunity to sneak to Jerome's house. My mom found out she was pregnant at age sixteen. She told her mother and they went to the clinic. The clinic doctor and her mother agreed that she was way too young to have a baby. Her pregnancy was terminated.

My mom continued to see Jerome. During her senior year of high school, she became pregnant with me. This time, Mom decided to keep the baby. She completed her senior year of high school. She and Jerome were married a week after their graduation ceremonies. She was smart, and she worked hard to earn good grades. Because of this, her parents supported her decision to get married. My parents were young, but they knew they were going to have a child together—Grandpa Billy and Nana's first grandchild. Family was everything to

Grandpa, and he wanted to support his daughter's decisions—even if he didn't care too much for his new son-in-law. He wanted his children, and grandchildren, to have a much better life than he had. He had dreams of providing for his family with a comfortable life.

After working for GM for a couple of years, on a modest income, the family was able to upgrade once again to a bigger home. This one was located on the south side of San Jose. This home was twice as big as the modest home on the east side. This time, with four bedrooms located in a cul de sac. The new home had a swimming pool in the backyard, and was located in a middle class neighborhood right down the street from a new computer plant called IBM.

Shortly after my mom and Jerome were married, they found a small apartment on the south side of San Jose. Things got off to an okay start. Mom found a part-time job at a retail store and Jerome also found a job to support his new family. My parents were still very young; they were still teenagers, now with more responsibility than either of them could really handle. They were both inexperienced when it came to relationships and marriage, and things didn't stay 'hunky dory' forever.

Reflection

Sometimes, where you come from has more influence over your life than where you're heading. I had to know where I came from to know where I was heading. My mother's parents were the matriarch and patriarch of the family. The way I was taught, and what I observed early on, gave influence over how I interpreted life and the people around me. My grandparents both had a great deal of influence over the decisions that I made. Both went through adversity and hoped to pass on positive ventures to their heirs.

Chapter 2

Old School

One of my earliest memories of my mom and dad's relationship drama was one time when my mom was getting me ready. I had to be about four at the time. She was combing my hair because her older brother, Keith, was on his way to take me to the aquarium along with his girlfriend and her daughter who was the same age. Keith was like a younger version of my Grandpa Billy, but you would never want to tell him that. He looked a lot like Grandpa and even carried himself like him. He had a good job at Lockheed Martin, a popular technology company in the Silicon Valley. He didn't have any children at the time, but his girlfriend's daughter was about the same age as me so sometimes we would have playdates.

This was going to be my first trip to an aquarium. I was so excited. I sat on a wooded bar stool, peering through the window in the living room that faced the street, as my mother combed my hair. Jerome was outside washing his car. All of a sudden, a red car swerved into the driveway. A lady jumped out of the car quickly, cursing at Jerome while he was washing his car.

"Why the fuck are you here?" he asked the lady.

"Tell her about us Jerome!" the lady screamed.

"Get out of here!" he yelled back. Jerome scurried through the front door. The lady was still screaming; then, my mom started yelling at the lady.

"Tell her Jerome! Tell her about us!" The lady continued to scream as Jerome tried to hold my mom back. I was scared and crying. The lady pulled out a knife, and then Mom grabbed a crow bar. As this was all going down, my uncle Keith happened to pull up just in time. Uncle Keith saw his sister and all the commotion and jumped out of the car. At some point, the lady took off. Then, Keith got into Jerome's face. A fight almost ensued; if it weren't for Keith's girlfriend, Cheri, and Mom holding the men back, it would have. Someone could have gone to jail that day. Even though all that went down, I still was able to enjoy my day at the aquarium.

Things weren't working out between my parents. The only connection they now had was a daughter. My mom surely wasn't going to stick around if Jerome couldn't be a faithful husband to her. They both had a lot of growing up to do.

Mom knew it was best for her and I to move back home with her parents. Their Southside home was a safe haven for Mom and her siblings. It was a second home to them. Even if they moved out, they knew they could always come back if need be. When my mom moved back home, her two younger siblings, Kenny and Melissa, still lived at home. Vanessa, my mom's older sister, had moved out recently so Mom and I took over her old room.

It had been five years since my parents separated. Even though we moved back home with Nana and Grandpa, that didn't mean that their relationship was over for good. Deep down inside, my mom was still in love with my dad. She hoped that, with a little time, he would mature and change his ways. Mom tried to forgive him and they continued to see each other. She became pregnant once again; this time a boy. They named him Andre.

My mother, brother, and I crammed into the smallest bedroom of my grandparent's house. They were now young parents with two small children. My parents started to rekindle their flame, but at a distance. Mom wanted to take things slow this time. Jerome found a better job and moved into his own studio apartment. Money was tight, but sometimes, as a family, we went out to pizza or to see a drive-in movie. Jerome even started taking Andre and I on weekend visits to his apartment. Even though he didn't have much food or furniture, I enjoyed spending time with him. He was like a big kid; Jerome played video games as I ate junk food. I mostly kept Andre entertained as he crawled and wobbled around the apartment. Dad didn't even have a couch, but he had a weight bench in the center of the living room. At his place, I was able to do all the flips and cartwheels I wanted— something I was unable to do at Nana and Grandpa's house.

The bliss ended when Mom found out Jerome was seeing someone else behind her back again. She was tired of the drama. They still tried to co-parent from a distance. Jerome was laid off from his job, and he expected my mom to understand. Money was tight on her end too. She worked as a data processor at a tech company that didn't pay very much. Jerome expected her to fit the bill for our expenses. He wasn't working. He expected her to understand his situation and pick up the slack.

Mom worked full-time and, many days, she had to work overtime just to purchase necessities for the three of us. After being laid off, Jerome came around less and less—until he didn't come around at all. A couple of years went by. I told myself that I didn't care whether or not Jerome was around. I told myself that I was glad that he wasn't. When he was around, he always ended up making my mom sad. Andre was now around four and I was nine. Jerome called mom and they talked for a while before she handed me the phone.

"Your father wants to speak to you," Mom said.

"Hello," I said in a shy, yet awkward way. It had been so long since I had talked to him, I hardly knew what to say or how to say it.

"Hey! How ya doing?"

"I'm good," I said coldly.

"I'm going to pick you and your brother up soon."

"Okay," I said.

"I'm going to take you to a baseball game. Don't you like baseball?"

"I guess," I said.

"What's your favorite team?" Jerome asked. I didn't really like watching baseball, but I knew Andre really liked to A's.

"I like the A's," I said.

"Well I'm going to pick you and your brother up and take you two to an A's game." At this time Andre started tugging at the phone.

"Let me talk to my dad," he demanded.

"Okay, well Andre wants to talk."

"Okay, I love you!"

"Love you too," I said as Andre snatched the phone from my hand.

"Daddy, I want to go to a baseball game! My favorite team is the A's! Like Tanisha!" Andre said without pausing in between words.

Eventually, the time came when Jerome had to tell Mom something. Jerome had another baby on the way. Shortly after, Jerome moved to Texas with the woman and his new baby. He had a job opportunity in Texas.

When Andre saw the A's play on television, he would say to me, "Dad is going to take us to a baseball game!" It had been almost a year since he told us that.

"No, he's not Andre," I said.

"Yes he is!" Andre shouted back. Andre was five, and I was ten years old. This became the norm. He never took Andre and I to that baseball game. The phone calls became fewer and fewer. Eventually, Jerome became virtually absent from our lives. He also wasn't helping out financially. After Jerome moved, it was many years before we spoke to him again.

Mom was always very detailed and organized. With those skills, she was able to get a job at an office performing clerical work. This new position paid more than her last job. If she saved her money she could finally afford to move out of Nana and Grandpa's home. This position fit her perfectly, but it was a full-time job and demanded long hours, a commute, and sometimes overtime. My grandparents helped out with watching us as much as they could. Nana had a lot of experience raising children. She raised five of her own after all. She and Grandpa Billy were in retirement, but they didn't mind assisting with childcare as much as they could.

I could tell that it was tough for Mom, being the sole provider and all. She came home from work looking stressed out and tired. It seemed like Mom was gone day and night working. During the week, she woke up before Andre and I. She left home before we were up for school. She got home when it was dark. I cherished the weekends because those were the only days I spent with my mother.

Grandpa Billy was like a second father to me. Just because my father wasn't around, he didn't want me to experience anything less than a great childhood. Grandpa had aged over the years, but he was still very handsome. Just more distinguished looking. He exercised regularly, but still hid a stash of candy in his sock drawer. I always knew where his candy stash was. He drove a 1972 Brown Lincoln Continental for the longest time. He purchased that car brand new.

He wasn't cheap, just conservative with his money. He spent his money on things that he thought would last and never cared too much about fads or styles. He had his own style and way of doing things.

In the evenings, Grandpa Billy watched CNN and spoke badly about the Bushes. "You know they are crooks!" I didn't know if he was asking me, telling me, or speaking to the television. He said, "the Bushes don't like blacks!" When he saw George Bush on television speaking, he usually turned the channel. When Grandpa was home, he didn't sleep much at night. He stayed up watching late night shows on cable.

On nice days, our family enjoyed barbecues in the backyard near the pool. Grandpa played his jazz music on the boom box while barbecuing. His favorite jazz selections were by artists, John Coltrane and Miles Davis. Sometimes they invited friends and neighbors.

"There are kids around. Why would she dress like that at a family barbecue?" my mom whispered to my aunt.

"That is just plain gross!" Melissa replied back quietly, with a stale look on her face. Keith's new girlfriend, Darlene, pranced around the pool in her red Brazilian cut bikini. Darleen was actually Keith's fiancé, but no one in the family really acknowledged the title that Keith gave her. The women of the family didn't care for her much. Darlene had a son named Adam who came along everywhere with her. Darlene had a beige complexion, thick eyebrows, and a round face with a pointed nose.

My aunt Melissa, Mom's younger sister, lived at the Southside house. Melissa and I were just twelve years apart. Sometimes, Melissa took me to the mall or to school with her. I looked up to her so much and thought she was the coolest. Her bedroom was painted pink, and she even had a day bed. Melissa's favorite music artists were Prince and Madonna, and she even had a boyfriend.

Grandpa Billy had been in California for decades, but still had a strong southern accent. He would grab my cheeks and pull my face close to his. Sometimes my nose touched his while he looked me close in the eyes and said, "You can do or be anything you chose."

My grandparents owned an RV and enjoyed traveling. Their RV was equipped with a bathroom, stove, oven, couch, pull out beds, and an air conditioner. They enjoyed the sights at the Grand Canyon and visiting casinos in Nevada. Sometimes, Andre and I were lucky enough to be invited to come along.

One summer, Nana and Grandpa took us on a trip to Omaha, Nebraska with them. We drove the RV across five states to get there. We were visiting Nana's younger brother, Jouse. Vernita's nephew, Jouse's son, was getting married and my grandma had to be there. When Jouse first called Nana with the news about the wedding, Grandpa Billy said that they couldn't go. Nana said that she was going with or without him. He knew it was important to her, but Grandpa Billy didn't care to go because, throughout the years, Jouse hadn't really made any effort to keep in touch with his sister. Nana's family didn't get along with Jouse's wife either. Nana's mother especially didn't like his wife. She called his wife, "That dark, ashy lady." Their mother thought Jouse was too good for the woman he married. On birthdays and holidays, there were no calls and the only time Nana talked to him was when she called. She happened to call. Jouse happened to tell her about the wedding, and Nana happened to want to go, even if that meant driving across country.

During the trip to Nebraska, we stopped at many destinations along the way. I peered out of the RV window as we drove down the interstate. I enjoyed the ride as I laid on the bed of the compartment above the passenger and driver's seat. When I looked out of the top window, I felt as if I were flying. As we drove, I peered through the top window overlooking the scenic views. We drove past the great salt lakes in Utah. In amazement, I watched the white, salty sand. I was mesmerized. The salt looked like sheets of white sparkles against the sun. Grandpa pulled over at a rest stop alongside the salt lakes, so that Andre and I could get a better look at them. We couldn't get out of the RV fast enough!

During the trip, we pulled over at another rest stop, and Grandpa Billy took the opportunity to say to me, "You know, Popo won't be here forever." Popo was the name he called himself. Grandpa Billy had brought something up that I hadn't really thought of. Grandpa was like my dad, and up until this point, I had never thought about the process of getting old and dying.

"Where are you going?" I asked innocently.

"Well, one day I'll be dead and gone," he said. I couldn't imagine anyone in my family dying or anything changing. I wanted these times in my life to last forever.

Our family wasn't very religious by any means. They attended church sometimes—usually on holidays like Easter Sunday, Christmas Eve, and maybe New Year's Day if it fell on a Sunday. Grandpa Billy didn't trust too many people and wasn't very fond of preachers either. He didn't like feeling pressured to give his money away. Every time he went to church, they asked for money. "The preachers at the pulpit preaching on Sundays are the same guys at the poker club smoking, gambling, and drinking on Friday and Saturday," Grandpa Billy said.

My auntie Vanessa attended church regularly—most Sundays. After Vanessa moved out, she picked me up from the South Side home to attend Emmanuel Baptist Church with her on Sundays. Vanessa dropped me off at the children's Sunday school, while she attended the regular church service in the cathedral. My favorite part of Sunday school was the singing. I loved music and loved to sing. My favorite church song was Jesus Loves Me.

Although I did like Sunday school, I was very curious about what they did in the 'big church' as I called it. One Sunday, Auntie Vanessa and I were running late to church service. I didn't want to attend the kids church; I wanted to go with her to the big church. Auntie Vanessa didn't have any time to argue, so she pulled me into the service with her.

The church choir sang loudly. There were people clapping their hands and stomping their feet. A brown man, with a mustache and goatee, walked up to the pulpit. He had glistening hair that curled past his shoulders and wore a burgundy robe. *Is this Jesus?* I thought to myself. I nudged Auntie Vanessa, "Auntie! Auntie! Is that Jesus?" I asked her.

"Shush!" Vanessa said back.

"Auntie, is it?" I pressed.

"Yes, now quiet!"

The man in the burgundy robe told the church congregation words from the bible. All the adults were mesmerized with what he was saying. I was lost and didn't know what the heck he was talking about. Then, the man on stage started jumping up and down, and in the background the organs blared. As his voice rose, the organs played louder. When he quieted his voice, soft music played in the background. It was all very dramatic and entertaining to me. Water dripped from the preacher's hair and onto the shoulders of his long, burgundy robe. The organs started to play louder and he raised his voice. He suddenly became very touched by what he was preaching about and tears started to roll down his cheeks. He then dropped to the ground, and his body started to convulse.

I was very concerned, but no one else seemed to be. "Is he ok?" I asked my aunt.

"Yes, he just caught the holy ghost, that's all." She said handing me a stick of gum. The deacons on the stage came up and carried the preacher away. Whatever he caught, I knew I didn't want to catch it. After that, I didn't want to go back to church with Aunt Vanessa.

Reflection

As a child, family was my comfort and backbone I grew up having comfort that, no matter what, someone always had my back.

Chapter 3

There's Levels to It

When I wasn't in school, I was with Nana. Nana had been a housewife for many years. When she wasn't taking care of the home, she frequented the shopping malls. "This is my exercise!" Nana would say. At a brisk pace, she'd walk around the mall in the mornings if it was too hot or too cold outside. During her exercise trips to the mall, she would buy something just about every time she went.

Nana owned many handbags of various colors, brands, and patterns. She also had many scarfs with various colors and patterns. When she didn't want to comb her hair, she would wrap her hair in a colorful silk scarf.

When I was bored and at home, I went into Nana's closet and played with her beautiful silk scarfs. I put a colorful scarf on my head and pretended it was long flowing hair. In her closet, besides clothes and shoes, I also found old pictures and cards, candy and poker chips. I would only look and place the items back neatly, just as I found them.

Nana kept her high school yearbook in her closet in a hatbox with other old photos. I Took the yearbook out of the hatbox and thumbed through the old black and white photos. The pictures were mostly of Caucasian students. It wasn't hard to find Nana; she was the only black girl in the photos. I located two photos of her. In one, Nana had her hair pulled back in a thick wavy ponytail. She was standing with two white girls who had thick black-rimmed glasses and short brown hair. Nana had a large smile on her face. I stared intently at the beautiful, smiling young lady in the picture. It was hard to believe that the young women in the picture was Nana. Time had changed her appearance.

Grandpa Billy merged onto the busy freeway. He was picking me up from school early that day because I had a dentist appointment. He put his blinker on and attempted to get over. A man in the car next to us wouldn't let him into the lane. Grandpa sped up and the car next to us sped up too. He rolled his window down and up his hand went out the window. The man in the car rolled his window down too and yelled out, "Nigger!" Grandpa Billy gave the guy the finger and yelled back with some choice words of his own.

I heard the urban form of the word used often. Grandpa used the word 'nigga' to describe other black men. My uncles used the urban N-word, nigga, between friends. I had also heard the word used in hip-hop song lyrics and movies. The other N-word, the one with the 'er', was the worst to say. This word was used by slave masters, Grandpa said. The word Nigger was taboo and was used in an attempt to belittle black people.

That day, in the car with Grandpa, was the first time I had heard another man use that word. I had also heard the word used at school— tossed around recklessly like a used rubber ball. The word was used to taunt me on a daily basis by a boy named Bruce. In my fourth grade classroom we had tables instead of individual desks. Obviously, Bruce wasn't happy with his seating arrangement, so he was going to make my time at school hell. He'd grab my pencil out of my hand as I wrote.

"You're nothing, but a nigger," he whispered.

"Stop it!" I would yell out.

"Tanisha, stop talking," my teacher would say.

"Yes, Ms. Z," I answered back. A few times, I was even given recess detention.

Before I could read, Nana read to me. The library wasn't too far away from the house. It was near the hospital about two miles away. Driving there took only five minutes. When I was old enough, Nana took me to the library. It was so exciting being able to choose my own books. There were so many books, it took me forever to choose. Nana walked off to the Romance aisle, leaving me in the Children's section. I enjoyed mystery and suspense stories. They didn't have many of those books in the children's section, so I would choose books in the teen section.

Nana was a great cook. She cooked large pots of spaghetti, casserole dishes, and soul food during the holidays. On New Year's Day, the family looked forward to a large pot of spicy gumbo, rice, and okra. On Christmas, black-eyed peas, corn bread, and collard greens. In the mornings, before school, Nana scrambles eggs and made toast or oatmeal. I sat in the kitchen next to the hot stove getting my hair pressed. Nana kept her home immaculate. There were no dishes in the sink. The kitchen floor was mopped. Nana vacuumed, scrubbed, and wiped daily. I was hard to find a speck of dust anywhere.

In the summer, I invited friends over to swim. Swimming was my favorite summer activity. After I was finished swimming, I enjoyed bathing in the sun. It usually wasn't until the sun had started to set that I was finished for the day. When I finally decided to come into the house, I was starving, sleepy, and at least three complexions darker. As I walked through the screen door leading in from the backyard, Uncle Kenny was standing in the kitchen with the fridge door open. The house was dim, but the fridge light illuminated the kitchen.

"Is that a ghost in here?" he said.

"Where?" I asked.

"Oh, Tanisha that's only you!" he replied. "It's so dark in here that I can only see your eyes!" said Uncle Kenny. He started laughing. Some occasions, he "playfully" called me 'blackly' and 'midnight'. He meant to be funny, but it wasn't always funny to me.

I didn't care that my Uncle Kenny warned me that if I kept swimming and lying in the sun every day that I would turn blacker than midnight. I also didn't mind that the chlorine in the pool mixed with the sun dried my hair out into a kinky afro. I didn't care until, Mom or Nana, depending on who was available, had to spend hours parting my hair into sections in order to comb through my curly kinks. After that, I spent another hour or two washing and blow drying my thick curly mane. Sometimes, Nana pressed my hair straight in the mornings before school.

We lived in a diverse part of town. People of various ethnic backgrounds and nationalities lived in the neighborhood. Many of the families had someone in the household who worked at one of the many technology companies in the area. Many of the neighbors had children. If one kid was outside playing in the front yard, another kid would come out to play too until there were many kids out playing. We road bikes, played in each other's front yards, and with our parent's permission, we played in each other's backyards.

I went to school with many of the children in the neighborhood. One evening, Grandpa Billy and Nana took their evening stroll after dinner. There weren't many black families in the neighborhood, so when they saw another black family, they felt the need to introduce themselves. The young family was from Nigeria. Come to find out, their youngest daughter was in the same class as me. The family lived just a few houses away. Tunji was tall and had dark skin. She had three older sisters and a younger brother. I enjoyed being around her large family. Tunji and I grew to be close friends. We played often. She came over often to swim or play Barbies. Tunji was easy going and enjoyed many of the same things I did. I loved Tunji's mother's cooking. She fried the best chicken. On special occasions, Tunji's mother made delicious Nigerian dishes. I liked the spices and flavor of the food.

In elementary school, the ethnic children were assigned to speech class even if English was their first language at home. My speech teacher was Miss Maloney; she was a tall lady with short dark hair and had an English accent. In speech class, I sat next to a little black girl named Tonia. Tonia and I were in the same grade, but different home room classes.

"Okay class, today we are going to focus on…Listen to me say the word students, then repeat after me… bobbin. I put the needle though the bobbin. BOBBIN!" We looked at each other and put our hands over our mouths and giggled. Tonia was new to our school. She was petite, had a light brown-sugar complexion, and brown slanted eyes like she was mixed with Asian. She spoke with a raspy voice.

The lessons in speech were a bit repetitive and boring. Tonia and I passed notes.

"What's so funny?" Miss Maloney asked.

"Nothing Miss Maloney," we replied. After that day, during the speech class, we became friends and passed time by making funny faces and passing funny notes to each other. I liked Tonia's silly personality. Tonia lived just around the corner from my grandparent's house. After school, I asked Nana if I could ride my bicycle to her house. Both of our mothers went to the same high school together. Tonia's mom was two years younger than mine.

I had a collection of Barbie dolls and I invited Tonia to come over to play. I had a vivid imagination and dreamed of living in a lavish mansion like Barbie. When playing Barbie dolls, my friends and I acted out long soap-opera scenarios of drama, love, and even some times tragedy.

"I love your outfit!" My Barbie with the long brown hair said to Tonia's Barbie. "I got to tell you something," my Barbie said.

"What is it?" Tonia's Barbie with blonde hair asked.

"I'm Ken's new girlfriend," my Barbie confessed. Tonia then took the blonde-haired Barbie she was holding and slapped the brown-haired one out of my hand. "Hey, why did you do that for?" I asked.

"Let's play something else."

"We just started playing."

"If we play, I want the bed."

"It's my new bed that I just got for Christmas!"

"Why do you get all the nice stuff, and I get all the raggedy things! She started to yell and scream. "You are no fair and we aren't friends anymore." She said with tears rolling down her cheeks as she stormed out the front door.

In the fifth grade, I became great friends with the neighbor's daughter. We were the same age, our brother's played together and that year we were in the same homeroom class. Every day after school, I would rush to get my homework done so I could play next door. When finished, I dashed through the front door and headed to the neighbor's house. On one day in particular, I knocked on the door and Heather, who happened to be white, barely opened it. "I can only have one friend here at a time," Heather said. At this point, I was confused, until a girl who looked kind of like me, walked out from behind Heather. Heather had traded me for another brown girl. My feelings were hurt, but at the end of that school year, Heather moved.

The next school year, the other brown girl Heather traded me for and I became friends. Her name was Porscha, like the car. Porscha and I had plenty in common. She had an easy going and free-spirited personality.

Mr. Fisher was rumored to be one of the meanest teachers at my elementary school, and I got him for a home room teacher. I was terrified on the first day of school. When my Aunt Melissa was in sixth grade, she had Mr. Fisher as a teacher. He was tall, with orange hair and freckles. Every day, he dressed like a basketball coach, always wearing a dress shirt and tie. Aunt Melissa said, "If you talk during his class you will have to stand on one leg the entire school day." Mr. Fischer was the only teacher who had a classroom in a portable. A portable was a classroom separated from the actual building on the school campus. Children were afraid of him.

After having Mr. Fischer as a teacher for a few weeks, I realized that he wasn't that bad. He was just a no-nonsense kind of person. Sometimes students tested his patience. One of the good things that came from being in Mr. Fischer's class was realizing my passion for writing and storytelling. Every morning, Mr. Fisher had us write in a daily journal. The journal was confidential. I was able to express myself in a creative way. One day, Mr. Fischer came into class and said, "Today class, you will have a chance to write and publish your own short story. You will write a 1000-word short, suspense story that will be made into a book." I was so excited! I took my story writing so seriously that I had Nana and my mom read and reread it to edit my work. At the end of the school year, each student received their own bound copy of the book.

The last day of sixth grade came and went. On the last day of class, Mr. Fisher cried like a baby and told us that we were the best students he had ever had. I realized that he wasn't mean, just very passionate about teaching. Many of the children that once lived in the neighborhood moved away or went to different schools. San Jose's population was expanding and some school children were bused to other schools across town.

Reflection

School is where I learned that I was different. Television and music taught me about the perception society had of me.

Chapter 4

Growing Up Too Fast

Before the days of the Internet, besides learning in school, children learned from exploring and watching T.V. I stopped asking adults questions. Instead of adults answering my questions honestly, they would go around and around instead of giving a straight answer. Maybe adults were afraid of what children would do with the new knowledge, or maybe they just didn't know the correct answers themselves. The best example of this was when I asked where babies came from; I heard some line about birds, bees, and storks before finding out the truth for myself. The curiosities of life led me to explore things on my own. In translation, being curious led me to snooping, and the willingness to try something at least one time before ruling it out.

I grew up watching shows like "In Living Color" and cable networks like BET and MTV. On television, I saw women of color portrayed as many things—mainly prostitutes, strippers, music video models, single welfare moms, and crack addicts. I can't recall any story lines from the past where a black woman was represented as the heroine who saved the day. She was mainly the victim of unfortunate circumstances. The images that I saw on TV that represented beauty were mainly of white girls or women and girls who were racially ambiguous, having fair skin. I realized that there weren't many girls on TV who looked like me. I questioned whether or not a girl who looked like me was beautiful.

Mom was still working a lot, and I hadn't seen or spoken to my father since before I could remember. On the weekends, Mom and I didn't go to the movies or spend much time together. Mom was starting to live her life. I never really questioned my father not being around; that was just the way things were. I always had enough family to keep me occupied and feeling loved.

That is, until Mom got a raise and, after years of living with Nana and Grandpa, we were finally ready to move out on our own. I assisted Mom in choosing the new place. The requirements: it had to be in a safe location, be within Mom's budget, and near the freeway. We found a small two-bedroom duplex down the way. It was small, but it fit the budget.

We were now settled into our new place when mom started dating again. Her new boyfriend was a fire fighter. Instead of sitting on the couch watching TV in the evenings or weekends, as she normally did, she became more outgoing. She started leaving Andre and I home alone more and more often. To me, Mom had started acting different. She was working out and dressing different; even eating different foods. She now spent her extra time with her new love interest.

Mom got a dial up connection to the Internet to help with homework. In order to search the net, we had to plug our computer into a landline phone connection. I didn't used the Internet much since it tied up the phone line. I hated to think that I may miss a call. I loved talking on the phone, and if someone attempted to call, they were left with a busy signal as long as I was searching the net.

The closest thing to social networking we had at the time was called 'party line. Party line was an 800 number that my friends and I dialed into to connect with other teens from various areas. There were various phone chat rooms where we talked with people from locations all over the country. Just a few people I connected with on the phone line were actually from the Bay Area. The party line didn't last too long after I racked up long distance phone charges. Mom put a long distance block on the phone and that was the end of party line.

Besides talking on the phone, I spent a lot of time listening to music. I listened to music artists like the late R&B singer Aaliyah and TLC. I embraced their 'tom boy' style of tight fitting boy shirts under overalls, baggy jeans, and Cross Colors clothing. TLC was known for wearing condoms pinned to their baggy, colorful outfits. I wanted to be like them so collected condoms even though I didn't go as far as pinning them to my clothes. I knew what condoms were used for, but I hadn't had sex yet so I wasn't using any of them. I had collected all kinds of condoms of various brands and packaging. I had Gold Circle condoms, where the package looked like a gold coin, colorful lollipop condoms, Trojan brand, and Life Style. Other students at school collected them too. So, I would trade or purchase them from convenience stores.

My collection was located in a little green plastic bin hidden in the back of my closet. One day, mom needed something out of my closet. The green bin filled with condoms slid off the shelf and almost landed on mom's head. The contents of the bin scattered all over floor. At first, Mom thought that the colorful contents were candy rather than condoms. When she took a second look, she knew exactly what they were. "Tanisha! Why do you have these?" She asked with a sad, yet disgusted, look on her face. Mom don't worry, I'm not having sex." I replied. She couldn't do anything, but believe me.

At age thirteen, all that mattered to me was my friends and what other people thought of me. I started hanging out with my friends more often. We had sleep-overs at one another's homes. One of my new friends—who I met in middle school—was a girl named Leticia. I met Leticia on the first day of seventh grade; she wore a royal blue spandex dress. She was Mexican, petite, with wavy long dark brown hair. She already started wearing makeup, and usually wore bright red or maroon lipstick with heavy eyeliner and mascara.

"Mom, can my friend Leticia spend the night?" I asked.

"Who's Leticia?" my mom asked. Mom couldn't keep up with all the friends I had met since starting middle school.

"The girl who wears the lipstick Mom." I replied. Many of my friends and I wore lipstick too, we just wiped it off before we got around our parents. Mom wasn't too comfortable with me hanging out with Leticia.

I made some new friends as well as some enemies. There weren't many black girls at my school. From a distance, this girl resembled a friend that I had known in elementary school. This friend had moved away, and I hadn't seen her since. As I got a closer look at the girl, I realized that it wasn't my friend after all. Like my friend though, this girl was bi-racial—Mexican and black—with brown skin and long curly hair. The girl, Laweeta, and I had PE class together. Maybe she saw me as competition, but it was no secret that she didn't like me. We had mutual friends in our PE class.

"Who do you think can run faster?" she asked our friends. One time, she asked, "Who do you think is prettier, me or Tanisha?" At the end of PE class, as I walked into the locker room, Laweeta was walking in at the same time. She came up and bumped my left shoulder and arm. "Oops, sorry," she said.

"You did that on purpose!" I had enough of her bad attitude and rudeness, so I pushed her back. She reached for my thick ponytail and I grabbed hers. This was the first fight I had ever been in. The PE teacher ran up and broke up the fight. We both got in--house suspension. We also had to sit out of PE the next day and, instead, had to clean the girls' locker room.

Tonia's mom, Dee, called Tonia and I Salt n' Peppa, after the music group. Dee was a young single mother, who worked two jobs to support her children.

"Why do you call us Salt N' Peppa?" I asked Ms. Dee.

"You and Tonia remind me so much of me and my friend Sharon. Like you two, we were best friends growing up. She was dark-skinned like you Tanisha, and we were both cute and they called us Salt N' Peppa." After Dee told me that story, it made me dislike the name even more.

When it came to us doing things and going places, Dee was a little more lenient than my mom. If I wanted to go somewhere that I didn't think my mom would approve of, I would ask to spend the night at Tonia's house. The skating rink on Friday nights was the place to be. Kids from all over town gathered there. The environment was very much different from that of school. There was no supervision. Parents just dropped off their kids for two or three sessions. The first evening skate session started at 6pm and went until 7:30pm. The second session started at 8pm and lasted until 9:30pm. My friends and I asked to be picked up at 10pm.

On my way out, a skinny dark-skinned boy with bucked teeth approached me, "Hey Ma, can I get your number?"

I was not interested and replied, "No thanks!"

The boy then yelled at me, "Fuck you then hoe! I don't like girls with braces anyway!" The crowd of boys with him laughed hysterically out loud. I was embarrassed and this upset me. I didn't know what to say or how to respond to the rude boy. I certainly didn't want to argue or fight with him. So, I looked away and said nothing.

"Are you sure you will be okay home alone?" my mom asked one day.

"Yes, Mom," I replied.

"Don't go anywhere! I will call to check up on you every hour or so. Make sure you have the ringer on."

"Mom don't worry." After a few hours of cartoons and talk shows, I was super bored. I figured that Mom didn't say I could have any friends over, so I called Tonia. Tonia arrived about a half hour later. I remembered the box that I had found in my mom's closet a while back. "Hey do you want to see something?" I asked. Tonia followed me to my mother's closet. There was a box and inside the box was a stash of VHS tapes. Right there on the front of the cover of the VHS box was a naked woman in compromising positions. I started to feel bad about snooping in my mom's things, but my curiosity outweighed my conscience.

"Do you want to watch it?" Tonia asked. I took the VHS tape out of the box and put it in the VCR and pressed play. Two women and a man sat in a hot tub. The three of them traded stories about their first time having sex. With every story, there was a new kinky scene. Seeing these images ignited a curiosity in me.

The next weekend, I asked mom if my friend Michelle could spend the night. Michelle had moved into the neighborhood a couple years back, but she and I didn't start hanging out until recently. Michelle was bi-racial—Hispanic and white. She had long, thick auburn colored hair that hung below her waste.

Michelle had a boyfriend named Carlos. She spent most of the night talking to him on the phone. As soon I got ready to turn out the lights, Michelle says, "I'm going to sneak out to see Carlos."

"What?!" I gasped. I felt a little used. Did Michelle spend the night, just so she could go see Carlos?

"Do you want to come?" Michelle asked. 'You can kick it with Dawn." Dawn was her boyfriend's best friend. I wasn't interested in Dawn. If I got caught, I would be grounded forever.

"No, I can't." Michelle ended up sneaking out of the house. She was never caught. Seeing Michelle sneaking out of the house gave me the idea that sneaking out of the house wasn't so hard after all.

On the weekends, my friends and I caught the bus to the mall. Mom was in her twenties, still petite, and had an eye for fashion. I snuck into her closet to wear her tight fitting body suites and costume jewelry. My friends and I left the house in what our parents thought were our everyday clothes, only to change into tighter fitting, scantily clad attire after arriving at our destination. As soon as we got to the mall, we would shoot to the bathroom where we would put on makeup and strip down to our sexy clothing underneath.

Me and Leticia were talking on the phone one evening.

"Are you a virgin?" she asked me.

"Umm...No!" I replied. I didn't know what virgin meant, but I knew it was an uncool thing to be one. Later that week, my mother was sitting on the couch watching an episode of Seinfeld. During this episode, Jerry sees an old girlfriend, Marla Penny, in a bar and mentions to George that when he last saw her, she was a virgin. Jerry asks her out and finds out that she was still a virgin. When I overheard, the word on TV, I took the opportunity to ask, "What is a virgin?"

"A virgin is a person who has not had sex." Mom said.

The next day, I confided in Leticia that I actually was a virgin and that I hadn't even made out or hooked up with a boy. I wanted a boyfriend, but didn't want to admit that I was a little scared. Letty was definitely interested in boys and boys were interested in her. She wore spandex dresses, tight pants, and very short shorts.

Every time we went to the mall boys, and sometimes even men, would approach Leticia. For me, the tom-boy look was cute, but got old fast. I wanted to get more attention from guys.

I walked to the drug store near my house. I had ten dollars that I saved from my lunch money. I found the aisle with the 99-cent make up and purchased black liner, a pressed powder compact, maroon lipstick, and Binaca Breath Spray because I liked the way that it tasted. I still wore body suites, but traded the baggy jeans for colored spandex jeans that zipped in the back or tight denim. Mom allowed me to finally get my hair straitened, and I started wearing it down more often.

Leticia was determined to hook me up with someone before the end of **eighth** grade. "I know a lot of fine black guys that would like you…I'm going to hook you up!" Leticia said. "My goal is to get you laid before the end of the school year." I was curious about kissing and maybe second base, but sex for now was way out of the question. Many of my friends were sexually active. It wasn't like it was a secret; many of them bragged about the boys they slept with or messed around. Some talked about performing sexual acts with multiple partners—many of these partners being much older than they were.

The next day at school, during lunch, Leticia came up to me and said, "I met this fine ass black guy at the mall!" She told the "fine ass black guy" that she had a boyfriend, but she did have a pretty black girlfriend to hook him up with. I was a bit reluctant about this arrangement. Later that day, after school, Leticia called me with the boy on three-way.

The boy, whose name was Michael, attended a high school nearby. He and I talked on the phone for weeks before I agreed to meet up with him. Finally, the day came when I decided to meet Michael. They were having a small carnival down the street from my house. I had it all planned out; I told Mom that I was going to meet one of my girlfriends at the carnival, but the whole time I planned on meeting Michael.

He was already there when I arrived. We were the only two black kids there, so it wasn't really hard to spot each other. He was tall, almost six feet, with a caramel complexion and braces, like me. He seemed pretty nice. He was just okay, not fine like Leticia had described. He had a big nose and braces. In my mind I thought, *Since I'm here we might as well just make out and get it out of the way.* We walked around the carnival and talked for a bit. He bought me a soda; I was way too nervous to eat. I spotted a corner out of everyone's view and grabbed his hand. "Come on over here!" I said. We were away from everyone now. He pulled me close to him and started kissing me with full on tongue. He then reached up my shirt and grabbed my boob. I was just kind of standing there. His hand unzipped my jeans. He shoved his hands into my pants.

It wasn't as romantic or glamorous as I thought it would be. I was still very nervous and had all kinds of thoughts running through my head. *Was I kissing the right way?* Less than two minutes had gone by when I stopped and told Michael that I heard someone coming. I pulled away and zipped my pants. Before that day, I had never kissed or made out. I had to call Tonia and Leticia to tell them all about it.

Dee normally worked Friday nights. One night, Tonia and I told our mothers that we were going skating. We had our parents drop us off at the skating rink. We decided that we would go back to Tonia's house and invite Michael and his friend over to the house once Dee left for work. Ever since we made out that day, he had been ringing my phone off the hook.

The skating rink was about a mile from Tonia's new house. My mom dropped me off at Tonia's so that Dee could drop us off at the skating rink before she went to work. Dee dropped us off and we had the boys meet us there. Then, me, Michael, his friend, and Tonia walked from the skating rink to her house. When we got there, at first we just sat on the couch, talking and hanging out.

Somehow, Michael and I made it from the couch to the bedroom. We started kissing and feeling each other up, then he pulled down my pants.

"I'm going to take your virginity," he whispered in my ear. I had told him that I was a virgin on the phone the other night. He was a little older than I was and wasn't a virgin. The pressure didn't feel as good as I had imagined. It actually really hurt.

I started to cry as I tried to push him off of me. It lasted about five minutes. He gave me a hug and kissed me on the cheek. I didn't feel good at all.

Mom and I weren't seeing eye to eye. She said that ever since I had started hanging out with Leticia, my personality changed. "I don't know about your friend Leticia; she's kind of fast," Mom said.

"Well, Mom you don't even know her!" I said back in a sassy voice. I thought to myself, *My mom doesn't understand me or my friends.* I started to miss not having my father around. Maybe if he was around, he would understand me better.

Tonia told me that her mom got pregnant after her first time having sex. I was now terrified and thought that I too could possibly be pregnant. It was difficult, but I decided that I would tell my mom that I had sex. So many things ran across my mind. *What if I was pregnant? What would I do?* When my mom got off of work that evening, I planned to tell her.

"Mom, I have to tell you something."
"What is it Tanisha?"

"I had sex with Michael." Mom was so disappointed, that she started to cry. She even contacted Michael's mom. This made me feel even worse. Mom made an appointment for me at the clinic. Luckily, I wasn't pregnant.

I told him that I couldn't have sex anymore. After that, he wasn't as eager to call me. The relationship lasted until I found out that he was seeing a girl at his school. Probably a girl who was giving it up. I broke it off with him. I was sad and felt used. I will admit, I wanted revenge. I was going to get another boyfriend to make him jealous.

Tonia tried to set me up with a friend of a boy she was talking to. I wasn't very interested in the boy though. Somehow, the boy that Tonia was talking to and I started talking on the phone. Tonia didn't know about the casual conversations that we were having. His name was Jon. One day after school, Jon and I met up. I was young, and I didn't think much of it. He went to the same school as Michael. Tonia said he was such a good kisser.

After meeting up with Jon, we sparked up a little thing for each other. I still didn't mention to Tonia that I was talking to Jon. Whenever she mentioned his name, which was often, I just didn't have a comment. I didn't mind that he liked both of us because he did like Tonia first.

One weekend, a mutual friend of ours from school spent the night at my house. While she was there, Jon called to ask if I could meet up with him a little later since his mom would be at work.

"Okay, my friend's mom is going to pick her up soon, and we can meet up after." I said and hung up the phone.

"Who was that?" asked my friend.

"That was Jon," I replied.

"Tonia talks to a boy named Jon. Is that the same boy?" She asked with big eyes and curiosity.

"Yes, why?" I asked.

"You're meeting up with him? Does your mom know?"

"Of course not! What's up with all the questions."

"Does Tonia know?" she asked.

"No, she doesn't know either."

I met up with Jon and later that evening, I received a phone call from Tonia.

"You betrayed me! How could you do this?" She sounded very pissed off at me. I started to feel bad. I tried to explain myself, but couldn't get a word in. I didn't know how this would impact our friendship. Rumors set in and news traveled very quickly. The next day I came to school and the energy was different. It seemed like everyone was whispering and talking about me. Some of it was true, other things were just lies or exaggerated. Tonia told everyone that I slept with her boyfriend. I had mutual friends that took her side and wouldn't speak to me. I felt like everyone was against me. Friends and even people I didn't know gave me the cold shoulder. Tonia even told some about the pregnancy scare that I had. I knew it was her because she was the only one I told besides my mom. Everyone was talking about it.

My friend Sophia was the only person who was still talking to me. Her family was from Samoa. She was tall, with olive colored skin and curly hair. She walked up to me on the way to history class and said, "Some girls are supposed to come up to the school tomorrow for you."

"What? Why?" I asked.

"I heard that a group of girls wanted to jump you because one of the girls heard that you messed around with her boyfriend." This was the same boy that Tonia tried to set me up with that day at her house. I knew exactly who those girls were. They wore khakis and blue like they were in a gang. They were all much taller and heavier than I was. I was very scared. When I came home after school, I felt physically sick. I decided that I wasn't going to school the next day.

The next morning, came and I told my mother that I had really bad cramps. I guess my excuse wasn't good enough because she told me that I couldn't stay home. "If you feel that bad when you get to school, go to the nurse." Mom said. She wasn't buying it.
I had lied to her before and she just assumed I was lying again. She wrote a note and handed me an aspirin before leaving for work. I gave her a sad look. Inside, I felt like this may be my last time seeing her.

"I'll have Grandpa pick you up and take you to school a little late," I guess the pathetic look helped a little.

Grandpa and I drove past the school in his dark brown, metallic 1976 Lincoln Continental Mark IV. I saw a group of black girls that went to the high school walking away from my middle school. I sunk down low in the passenger seat. "Who you hiding from?" Grandpa asked with a frown on his face. *Oh no*, I thought to my-self; so I made up a quick fib. "No one Grandpa. I just don't want anyone to see me come in late to school, that's all."

"Okay well, always sit up straight and never be ashamed of anything!" Grandpa said. Pulling up to the curb in the front of the school. He then said, "Have a good day! Popo loves you!" *He is so embarrassing!* I thought to myself. Even though it was embarrassing, Grandpa made me smile.

"I Love you too Grandpa!" I replied.

The girls that wanted to jump me didn't come up to my middle school again, and eventually my friends started to talk to me, like nothing ever happened. Tonia and I eventually made up, but our friendship seemed different. Middle school was finally over. I vowed to myself that I would make better choices from now on. I didn't want to be in the middle of school drama, especially in high school. But, my bad decisions seemed to haunt me.

Since I told Mom that I was having sex, she had me on restriction. As much as I knew, I was on punishment for the whole summer. The only thing Mom gave me permission to do was go to summer school and nowhere else. I was on "restriction" often these days, as mom called it. I called it "lock down." She made sure that I couldn't talk on the phone and didn't go anywhere except school. I felt like I was in a prison camp.

"Sorry Michelle, Tanisha can't talk on the phone; she is on restriction." When Mom told my friends that, it drove me crazy.

After day one home from summer vacation, I was bored. I felt alienated from all of my friends. I watched a lot of T.V—one of the few things I wasn't grounded from. I mainly just watched talk shows, music videos, and late night television. Unless, Nana picked me up to go with her to the mall or shopping center, I mainly stayed indoors listening to music, writing in my journal, and drawing.

Mom was spending more time with her new beau. He worked for the San Jose Fire Department and because of that, my family was all smiles and giggles when he came around. I didn't know for sure if they liked him for his personality or his job. I didn't care what job he had, I wasn't fond of him at all. Mom had changed since getting with him. She was becoming a person I didn't recognize. Since meeting Malik, Mom got on this health kick—working out and doing aerobics. Mom was going out more without me and spending more time away from home. Some days, she even slept over her Malik's house at night, leaving me home to watch Andre. Sure, I was old enough to take care of my brother, but I felt like Mom was starting another life without us.

A couple of weeks later, summer school started. I was so excited to take high school classes and even happier to finally get away from the house.

I had a good day at summer school. I enjoyed the teachers. I did see one of the girls who was in that group who came to my school looking to jump me. Later on, at the end of the school day, Tonia and two other girls from the group who wanted to jump me came up to me as I was leaving summer school. I had only been in one fight and it was one-on-one. I was scared of getting jumped. I walked away. Tonia walked away with the girls. The next day, I didn't go back to summer school.

I wanted to sneak on the phone to make a call to one of my friends, so I picked up the phone and once again, Mom was talking to Malik on the phone. As they talked, I listened in for a moment.

"You just need to be stricter," Malik said.

"This is just so stressful. I don't know what to do with this girl. She's out of control and having sex."

"Take everything away from her—take the phone away, and have her come right home after school," Malik replied.

I was so angry with her. I couldn't believe that she had the audacity to tell this man my personal business like that. For a moment, I thought about saying something or slamming the phone down, but I knew that was going too far. I quietly hung up the phone so she didn't know I overheard her and Malik's conversation. I felt that every punishment was his idea, not moms. Before her new boyfriend came along, she never treated me this way.

Because of those girls, I refused to go to the high school near the house. Mom agreed to enroll me in another high school; she just got tired of hearing about the drama. She took a day off of work and requested that I have an inner-district transfer.

I stopped asking to use the phone or go places. Mom figured that I had learned my lesson and took me off of punishment. I stopped asking because I no longer wanted to go anywhere. For the remainder of the summer, I sat in the house watching a lot of TV. Mainly music videos—Music Videos on cable networks like BET and MTV—and stayed up watching a lot of late night TV.

One thing my mom wasn't aware of was how I was really feeling. I didn't feel like I had anyone I could talk to. I felt so sad and alone. One day, I grabbed a new razor out of the package that I got to shave my legs. I started cutting my wrists. I used a bandage to cover the cuts. I knew that I wouldn't die. This was just a way to release my sadness.

Reflection

I was told once, "Life is not a race, but a briskly paced marathon." It wasn't until later in life that I understood that quote. Like many teenagers, I thought that I had life figured out. I saw things the way I wanted to and attempted to live under my own terms. Although many call my personality type strong-willed, and I still am, I was just like most teenage girls who want to explore life. I wasn't completely out of control.

Middle school was a turning point in my life. My mother didn't want her daughter to end up making a life changing decision that she may one day regret. I wasn't fortunate enough to have answers to information at the touch of a button. I learned by exploring life. My early teen years is when I started to get rebellious and test my individualism. Many of my friends grew up fast and when I hadn't yet, I felt like a minority—like, if I didn't, I wouldn't be accepted.

Sometimes I was angry with my mother about working so much. But, at the same time, I understood that Mom had to pay the bills. In translation, I was mad that my other parent wasn't around to share the burden with her. I started to take my frustration out on the closet person to me, and at the time, that was my mother and myself. I didn't understand the bigger picture and what she experienced or how hard she actually worked. I started wanting to spend less time with family and more time with others. I learned from the mistakes that I made in the past and just wanted the freedom to live and make decisions on my own. So, instead of asking my mother, I decided not to tell her anything. I was determined to figure things out on my own.

I became starved for attention; the times I felt I needed her most, she was either working or out with her boyfriend. I started to feel unloved and left out and believed that she was saving the best of herself for her boyfriend. This was the first time that I started to miss my father not being around. As I approached my teenage years, I felt resentment towards my mother. So, like most teens, this resentment turned into self-destructive behavior. Once, after a heated argument with Mom, I grabbed a razor that I used to shave my legs and started slicing at my wrists. Although I knew that I wasn't going to actually slice my vein, I knew that I would get attention from my mother.

On top of all the insecurity I was already feeling, being exposed to such an unflattering portrayal of a group of people that were supposed to represent me and my culture was very confusing to me as a young person. On one hand, I had dreams and ambitions to be successful, but on the other hand, I had this image of what society really thought of black girls and it made me questions myself constantly.

Chapter 5

My Stilettos: Finding Balance

It was the beginning of freshmen year in high school. I was on a much better track than last year. I was focusing more on school and left the boys alone, for now. One day, while listening to the radio, an advertisement about a modeling and talent search came on; it was being held the following weekend. The ad said that a casting agency was looking for teens and adults, fourteen to twenty-one years of age, to be featured in magazines and television. I had always wanted to be on television. I imagined opening a fashion magazine and seeing my face in an advertisement. The agency was holding the casting call at a hotel right up the freeway from my house. I convinced my mom to take me.

Mom and I arrived at the large hotel just a few miles down the highway from our house. It took us awhile to find a parking space, but once we found one, we walked into the large lobby. Even though there were many people there, it was still quiet; so quiet that my shoes made an echo as I walked. There was a sign that read, "Welcome! Casting Call." The sign had an arrow that pointed to the left. There was a small line of two to three people behind a card table that a lady sat behind while they signed their names on a clipboard. There were others in the large banquet room, which was lined with chairs that were filled with anxious bodies waiting for their turn to speak with a casting agent.

Earlier that morning, it took me awhile to find just the right outfit to wear. I changed about ten times before deciding to wear my black and blue denim dress. It came slightly above my knees, but it didn't make me look too grown. My hair was down; Mom helped me straighten it. I wanted to get my makeup done at the mall like Mom had when she went out for her thirtieth birthday, but she said, "That would make you look too grown!" So, I just did my regular: mascara, liquid liner, pink lip gloss, and a touch of blush. Mom suggested not to overdo it.

When it was my turn, I nervously walked up to the card table. I was given a number and told to take a seat. Once they called my number, I was ushered into a room and Mom stayed in the waiting area. In the room, there was a video camera on a tripod set up. A lady dressed in a grey suite began to ask me a series of questions, as a man behind the camera filmed.

"Hi There! What's your name?" the lady asked. "What school do you attend? What brings you to the casting today?" My palms started to sweat. That happens when I'm nervous. This was my first time at an audition, and I felt a little awkward. I started to feel a lump swell in my throat.

After I answered the questions, the lady asked me if I had any talents. I had to think for a moment. "Well, in sixth grade and eighth, I was a cheerleader for youth football. I can do the splits and sing a little!"

"What can you sing?" The lady asked.

"Gospel or patriotic," I went with the patriotic sound and started with the Star Spangle Banner. "Oh say can you see…" Luckily, she cut me off before any high notes.

Later in the evening, Mom received a call from the agency. Mom had a huge smile on her face when she handed me the phone. The voice on the other end said, "Hi Tanisha?"

"Yes," I nervously replied.

"You have been chosen out of hundreds of applicants for a call back tomorrow. Please bring with you an 8x10 photo and dress casually. Congratulations!"

The next day, mom and I went to the hotel once again; this time to go over the contractual details of the school and casting agency.

"We think your daughter has what it takes to get into modeling and acting." Even though the guy talked about how they guarantee that they help find me the first paid gig, Mom's face dropped.

"Does this mean we have to pay for this?" She asked in a disappointed tone. Mom got up and said, "Thank you, have a great day." I sadly followed behind my mom.

The guy got up a said, "Wait! Here's what we can do. We can provide Tanisha with a partial scholarship, and you can make payments for the rest." She thought about it for a minute; she knew how important this was to me. She finally agreed!

I was given an exciting opportunity to join modeling and acting school. I was to attend class in San Francisco every Saturday for six months, then after we would have a graduation ceremony. The classes were a full day, starting at 8am and ending at 4pm. There were about ten students in the class. In my class, the students were of various ages between fourteen through twenty-one years of age. The first class I attended, I was so nervous. We were in a room with bright lights, white walls, and mirrors on one side. The instructors taught us how to walk on a runway, act, pose during a photo shoot, and apply makeup. We even had a two-day photo shoot to develop a portfolio and zed cards.

Every Saturday, mom and I drove to San Francisco. It was just her and I spending time together. We had to hunt for parking on the packed city streets. Once we finally did find parking, we had to walk, what seemed like miles, to get to the building where my class was being held.

After several months of commuting on the weekends, I graduated from the acting school. We had a fantastic ceremony. The students put on a fabulous show for our parents and family. It was now time to look for work!

Mom and I didn't know the first place to start looking for modeling or acting jobs. Mom's friend at work had a daughter who modeled, and she suggested that we take my portfolio to local agencies. Not too long after, Mom and I took my portfolio and zed cards and visited a couple agencies. Two of the agencies critiqued my portfolio and said that I needed some variation in my look. One agency offered to redo my portfolio for a fee. Mom didn't have the money to invest any more into this. The last agency said that I wasn't the "look" they were currently seeking. Once I graduated from modeling school, I thought it would be easy to land a job, but that certainly wasn't the case.

A couple months later, one Sunday afternoon, Mom received a call from the school's agency. It was regarding a casting being held at the school. The agent who spoke to my mom said that the producer was looking for a young African female around my age to play a role for a movie being produced for a large TV network. The movie was based in 1963 when a bomb exploded during Sunday morning services at the 16th Street Baptist Church killing four young girls. The role sounded so sad. I didn't think about the sadness too long. When Mom told me about the conversation, I was so excited! I thought to myself, *This is my big moment!* The agency wanted us to meet the producer and audition to play one of the little girls who was burned in the Birmingham Alabama Church. The catch we had to make it there before 4pm. It was now 2:30pm. San Francisco was forty-five minutes down the freeway.

"Why would they call us at the last minute for something like this?" Mom complained as she scrambled to get dressed. Then, I couldn't figure out what to wear. Mom was in the middle of washing clothes. When we left the house it was five minutes after 3pm. I held onto my portfolio and zed cards tightly. I remembered what my acting school teacher told us about bringing them to every audition or casting call. Mom and I raced down the freeway. Approaching the city, there was some minor traffic that slowed down our trip.

It was now 4:05pm. Even thought it was peek time, Mom agreed to use up her minutes on her cell phone to call the agent.

"Hi, we are just looking for parking and we'll be right up!" Mom said. Mom had him on speaker phone.

"I'm sorry Lisa, but the casting director is no longer seeing applicants and is heading back to the airport now. Tanisha's appointment was at 4:00pm." Disappointed, my mom hung up the phone. I was so discouraged by the news. Mom was more pissed that she wasted a tank of gas and her Sunday afternoon. When I got home that evening, I packed my portfolio away. I thought maybe my acting and modeling career was over before it even began.

The bleachers were nearly empty, but there was supposed to be a pep rally being held in the gym in a few minutes, so the PE teacher let us out of class early. I sat by myself in the freshman section near the top of the bleachers. My high school was huge in comparison to my elementary and middle school. I attended Santa Teresa High School, located in the suburban southern region of San Jose. There were over 2000 students. It was freshman year, and I didn't know anyone at this large school. I only recognized a few familiar faces from middle school. No one that I had ever hung out with. I was relieved that I didn't have any enemies here, and I no longer felt like I had to watch my back. I wanted to make a new start. Friends that I went to school with like, Porscha and Tonia, went to schools closer to their new homes. Towards the end of 8th grade, Leticia found out she was pregnant and was going to a continuation school this year, and Michelle moved to Antioch.

As more and more students piled into the school gym, I noticed a girl that I had a class with walking up the bleachers. She had brown skin and looked Mexican. She had large brown eyes, long eyelashes, and dark brown almost waste length black hair. The girl came to where I was sitting and sat down. I looked up and gave her a closed-mouth, half smile. "Hey, I'm Shylia. What's your name?" she said politely.

"I'm Tanisha," I replied. I thought that it was a nice gesture for her to introduce herself like that. From then on, we became friends.

Like many high schools at Santa Teresa, kids of the same ethnicities clicked together. There were also cliques that had other associations besides race; there were jocks (students who were good at sports), smart people (who were generally all Asian), Cheerleaders hung out with cheerleaders, and most of the black students all gathered together no matter what their association was. The blacks gathered in their designated area, even if we had never spoken to one another. There weren't many black students, but the ones who went to my school were enough fill up the quad area near the cafeteria.

Shylia and I started hanging out together. Come to find out, she wasn't Mexican at all; she was middle eastern and her family was from Bangladesh. Shylia had a younger brother about the same age as mine. During lunch, we kind of hung out towards the edge of the quad area closer to the cafeteria. Some people actually would come up and often ask Shylia, "Are you black?"

"Why? If I wasn't would I not be allowed here?" She'd reply. After more than one person asked, we just told them that we were cousins and that Shylia was from Egypt. People actually bought it.

I met two other girls, Maureen and Katie. They both were in three of my classes. Art, math, and we were lab partners for science. We spent so much time in the three classes together that we couldn't help but to become friends. Katie had short, almost black hair. She was a cute girl. I think she was bi racial—Mexican and white. Towards the middle of the school year, she started to wear white face makeup and red eye shadow around her eyes, even though Maureen and I suggested that was a fashion no-go. I guess Katie wanted to make a statement and be different. Maureen was tall and blonde with braces. She was great at drawing. She doodled all these great artwork pieces on the margins of her note book.

When I celebrated my fifteenth birthday, I invited Maureen, Katie, and Shylia over to have a sleepover. We had so much fun eating pizza and watching scary movies. We stayed up late laughing and joking. It felt good just to be a kid and not trying to grow up too fast.

Shylia and I became great friends and started to hang out a lot. We liked the same music, clothes, and even had similar taste in boys. When we got to know each other more, I asked Shylia one day, "Are you a virgin?" She was a virgin and never had a boyfriend.

"Are you?" she asked.

"Yes, I'm a virgin," I said. I thought it was best not to tell anyone about my experience with boys. If I had told her, I'm not sure what she would have thought of me. Shylia and her family were of the Muslim faith. In her religion, it was important for her to stay a virgin until she was married. Her grandfather stayed home. When I came over, often he was in the living room praying. Shylia's house smelt of curry and sweet spices.

Shylia's mother and father both worked. After school, when they were at work, we found the keys to her father's old Volvo. Her dad had her start the car from time to time so that the battery wouldn't die. We decided that her dad would never notice if we took the car out for a spin around the neighborhood. We took turns driving around the neighborhood. When we were finished, Shylia parked the car nicely by the curb like she found it. Every day after school we looked forward to taking the car on a drive around the neighborhood.

When I bought something that Shylia thought was cute, she would ask her parents and the next day she would have the exact same thing. This started to annoy me a little, but at the same time, it was endearing. Shylia's dad eventually found out she was taking the car. Around that same time, her dad also found out she liked boys—black boys. It was a wrap after that. Her mother and father put her on lock down; she couldn't go anywhere, have company over, or talk on the phone.

I didn't really participate in any high school sports. Once, I thought about trying out for the basketball team, and I actually tried out for the song and dance team. The song and dance team was like the cheer squad, but instead of cheering, they focused more on dance routines while the cheerleaders focused on drills and formations. Song team members specialized in lyrical and jazz dancing. Most of the girls on the team had years of lessons. I thought that I had a chance to make the squad since I cheered for two years when I was younger, and I was an okay dancer. I guess that wasn't enough because I had an awful time remembering the choreography for the tryouts. I couldn't get the dance moves to save my life. After practicing day and night for the tryouts, I finally learned the choreography. I auditioned, and the next day they revealed the names. There was a list taped to the gymnasium wall; it included the names and grade level of the girls who made the team. My name wasn't on the list.

Shortly after, I got an opportunity to be a part of a non-school affiliated drill team. A friend's mother called my mom one day and told her she was starting a drill team. My mom thought it was a great idea and committed me to the team before asking me. The drill team had a total of ten girls. We wore white boots with tassels on the laces and had dance costumes specially made for each performance. We marched and performed dances in local parades and shows. I was also part of the Black Student Union at school. In the union, a few other girls and I formed a small choir. We sang in school rallies and other school events.

With my free time, I eventually got a part-time job working at a snack bar at a large local car dealership. My goal was, once I turned sixteen, to have my driver's license and a car. I found the job through Grandpa. A good friend of his owned a catering company. They owned the snack bar at the dealership. On Saturdays and Sundays, I worked for five dollars an hour preparing food, wiping counter tops, and sweeping floors in the hot sun. Although, the job was boring, and I disliked working on the weekends, I liked earning the extra money. I didn't have to ask my mother for bus money or money to buy food, and I was able to save for a car. I slowly earned my mother's trust back along with my freedom. When I turned sixteen, I got my driver's license and Grandpa cosigned so that I could purchase a car. It was just me and the open road now. I thought this was the beginning of my life as an adult.

Since starting high school, I had met many people. I met a lot of boys. Wherever I went, I was approached by a boy who wanted my number. I didn't want to be fast anymore; plus, I remembered what Grandpa taught me, "Don't get to know a person by what they tell you, observe the person's actions and how they treat others." Most boys just wanted one thing. For now, my focus was school and making a little money.

High school went by so quickly and before I knew it, I was a senior. I knew that I wanted to attend a college. I had enough credits to graduate early, but mom wouldn't let me. She said that I needed to be in school and figure things out. I joined the office experience program, where I learned about various office tasks, as well as taking math, language arts, and economics classes. I just had four classes and was finished with school every day before noon.

When anyone asked me what I wanted to major in when I went to college, I told them Dermatology. I wasn't really sure if I actually wanted that to be my major, or if in fact that was even a major at all. It sounded good at the time, and I knew dermatologists made good money—or at least that's what I read when I did my senior career research project at the beginning of the school year. To become a dermatologist, would mean to commit to a lot more school than I was sure I wanted to commit to. I honestly wasn't sure what I wanted to do for the rest of my life.

Mrs. Navarro was my Language Arts teacher. My new friend, Rachael, and I both had Mrs. Navarro's class together. Rachael had transferred from a private school the year before and played basketball. I didn't care too much for sports, but I was very competitive when it came to grades. Rachael had a beige complexion and curly hair that she wore pulled back into a thick pony tail. Rachael's dad was black and her mom was Mexican. Come to find out, Rachael was just as competitive as I was when it came to grades.

Mrs. Navarro also taught Literature at DeAnza College in the evenings. Every day, Mrs. Navarro had us do some creative writing piece. Rachael and I would be the first to complete our writing assignments. She starting giving Rachael and I the same work she gave her evening college students. I enjoyed writing poetry and essays. Mrs. Navarro even invited me to come visit one of her evening classes. "If you like it, you can enroll in the class next semester and earn college credit!" said Mrs. Navarro.

Beth was good friends with Rachael, and she too had transferred from the private school to Santa Teresa. Beth's mom was white and her dad was Mexican, but didn't look it. Her dad had reddish-brown hair. Beth had thick wavy hair that hung past her waist and green eyes.

Maya was another friend who Rachael had grown up with and lived near. Recently, since Rachael had started to hang out with different friends, they began to have problems. Maya didn't like Rachael new friends.

"Why don't you want to hang out with all of us?" One day on our way to lunch, Beth and I caught Rachael arguing with Maya outside of class.

"All you want to do is hang out with boys!"

"That's not true! Boys try to hang out with me." Rachael shouted back.

"The only reason why guys talk to you is because of your light skin," Maya said.

"Guys talk to Tanisha," Beth intervened.

"That's just because she has long hair." Maya shot back.

After all the years of wearing my hair long, I decided to cut my hair above my shoulders to prove a point that guys didnt only talk to me because I had long hair.

Senior year, we were much too young for night clubs, but my friends and I sat in the parking lots of concerts and other events. They called it, 'parking lot pimping,' also known as loitering. Every year, the local radio stations like KMEL, put on a concert called the Summer Jam. This was a concert where both local and popular artists performed. After spending some time in the parking lot of the concert, we decided to go to a local club downtown. It was a teenage club and many people leaving the concert said that's where they were heading. The club was located near the university, downtown. There was no alcohol served there, just juice and soda. There were so many young people out. We pulled up to the night club and as soon as I got out of the car, I spotted a cute guy. He wasn't very tall but, he was very handsome. He had a beige complexion, an athletic build, and a nice dimpled smile. I had recognized him from the Oak Grove vs. Independence high school basketball game earlier in the year. He was really good at basketball and scored most of the points. I knew that he was at least a year older than me. He disappeared into the crowd. "Let's go inside!" Rachael said and grabbed my arm.

My curfew was 12:00 on the weekends, and it was just about that time. We were just about to leave when a group of guys walked towards us. The guy that I spotted earlier was one of them. "Do you know what time it is?" the cute guy asked as Rachael and I walked past. I smiled. I knew someone in his group had a watch, cell phone, or pager. I told him the time, and he asked me my name. I asked him his and he said, "J.B." We exchanged numbers and starting talking on the phone that night. My stomach was full of butterflies when I talked to him. He was cute, and charming, but I wasn't going to meet up with him in the wee hours of the morning as he suggested. I found out that he recently graduated from high school, and was leaving to college soon.

"Since I'm leaving to college soon, you should come over," he hinted.

"Maybe tomorrow after work."

"It's a date!" J.B. lived on the other side of town. He lived in the nice part of town called Evergreen. The area was known for its lush green hills and large single family homes. When I pulled up to JB's house, he met me out front. He must have been watching out the window as I pulled up and parked.

"Do you like my car?" he asked. Parked in the driveway was a 5 series BMW with gold twenty inch rims and burgundy paint.

I never knew anyone as young as we were to have a car like that. I was impressed. He invited me inside his house. No one was home, but him. The house was big, but I could tell that it missed a woman's touch. There were trophies in all areas of the house. Mail and papers scattered across the dining room table.

"You sure have a lot of trophies," I said.

"I grew up racing BMX bikes, but I stopped a few years ago." His trophies were scattered around the house. The house itself was a little dusty and cluttered. JB showed me what he called his "trophy room." It was an extra bedroom with hundreds of trophies he had earned throughout his BMX racing and basketball career.

He then took me into his room. "To see my room means you're royalty," I started laughing—not only was he cute and rich, but he was funny. He had bunk beds in his room with names carved into the wood, posters on the wall and a beautiful view that over looked San José—all of the Santa Clara Valley actually.

"Maybe one day I can help you clean your room," I told him. I noticed his dimpled smile. It made me blush.

"I'll take you up on that, only if you do something for me."

"Cleaning up your room is doing something for you." I looked at him, and we started kissing. The next thing I remember was clothes coming off and me on top of him.

A couple of days later, we had one of those freak California storms and it was raining out. I was chilling at JB's house, watching a movie, when I received a text message. It was a guy that I had coincidently met the same night I met JB. I talked to him on the phone a few times, nothing serious. Before I had a chance to read the text, JB snatched the phone out of my hand. He demanded to know who was texting me. I was taken back by how he reacted to me getting a text.

"Just a friend!" I snapped back. There had been a few times that he had gotten calls or text messages from girls when I was around. When he did, he claimed the calls were just friends. He read the text and demanded to know who it was. "He's a guy that I met over the summer. I told him that I had a boyfriend and we're just friends. He calls to say hi."

"Call the number, I want to talk to the dude!" I thought that would be so unnecessary and embarrassing. So instead, I lunged after him to grab my phone.

"Give me my phone!" I yelled. JB pushed me off of him and onto the floor. Then, a wrestling match ensued between the two of us. When I finally got a hold of my phone, I grabbed my purse and stormed out of his house. I couldn't believe what had just happened. I vowed that I was done with him.

We made up and before I knew it, we were seeing each other daily. I went home, slept, got up, and was back at his house in the morning. When we weren't together, we talked on the phone. On late summer nights, we parked in the grassy fields near his house and made out in the back seat of his BMW.

He lived with his father and little sister, ten years his junior. He and his sister had different mothers. His mom was a nurse; she lived and worked in the East Bay.

J.B.'s father was a mechanical engineer who, on his spare time, raced cars. I called him Mr. Barnes. Grandpa taught me that it was polite to call elders 'Mr.' or 'Mrs.' unless they told me otherwise. Mr. Barnes was born and raised in the Midwest. It wasn't hard to tell where JB got his good looks and charm. Mr. Barnes was cool a parent. He seemed pretty easy going. He ordered take-out every night and didn't mind me being over so much. The beginning of the school year was starting and JB talked about going away to college, but it didn't seem like his plans were going through. I never really asked him what college he was going to—all I knew was that it was located in Florida.

Mr. Barnes was funny and always had an opinion about his son. He grew up in Kansas City, Missouri before moving to California in his twenties. He spoke with a Midwestern accent.

"So Tanisha, what are you doing with a chump like my son?" He asked. I didn't know how to answer that, so I just giggled. Mr. Barnes continued, "This chump was supposed to be going off to college, but lost his scholarship because he wanted to act a fool and got himself caught running away from home."

"I didn't lose my scholarship, Dad. The guy from admissions just called me the other day," JB replied.

"Your chances of playing for that school are over," said Mr. Barnes.

Rachael and I walked to class one morning as we usually did. Maya walked up to Rachael, "Bitch! Why are acting like you didn't hear me?"

"Who are you calling a bitch? Bitch!" said Rachael. Rachael and I started to walk off without saying anything else to Maya.

"What's that all about?" I asked. Before Rachael could answer, Maya stuck her foot out and tripped Rachael. Rachael couldn't catch her footing and fell to the ground as Maya jumped on top of her and started punching her in the face. I dropped my backpack on the ground and grabbed Maya by the hair, then I slapped her in the face. She quickly got up and ran off holding her eye. There was a group of kids surrounding us, but luckily no teachers. Rachael got up, quickly trying to dust herself off. She had dirt all over. I tried to help her pick the twigs and dead grass from her hair.

"Are you okay?" I asked.

Yeah, I'm fine," said Rachael. We washed up in the bathroom and went to class.

To get an early start, I took the practice SAT test in tenth grade. Now, I was getting ready to take the actual SAT during my senior year. I had already applied to five colleges and universities: Morgan State, San Jose State, San Diego State, Chico State, and USC. I applied to Morgan State after talking to my father. He had recently called. It had been so long that couldn't even remember the last time I had spoken to him. He recently moved to the East Coast and was expecting another daughter. He wanted to see me and suggested that I apply to college close to him. I researched schools and found out that Morgan State was in Maryland, so I applied. I applied to San Jose State as a backup plan. It was everyone's first choice at my high school, and I didn't want to make it mine. San Diego State was my third choice. *San Diego is a nice place*, I said to myself. Once I went to Sea World with my mom, aunts, uncles, cousins, and grandparents. We had a blast. Since it made a good vacation spot, it would probably make a fun place to go to college. Chico State was known for being a party school. The warning was: If you went there, you would party so much that you couldn't get any of your work done. There was a good chance you would fail out of school; my curiosity made me apply. Lastly, I applied to USC because JB said that was his second college choice just in case Florida A&M fell through. Florida was way too far, but just in case things worked out between us, I wanted the option to be close to him. I was accepted to all of the schools I applied for.

One week in office class, we typed our resumes. Mr. Chapman, my counselor and office teacher, was arranging a job fair. We would interview with real businesses. I maintained my grades, and was a part of the magnet program. Because I was in the magnet program, I got out of school before lunch.

I had just arrived at JB's house, and once again, we headed to the basketball courts at the park. Since meeting JB, my schedule had been nothing but school, work, his house, then to the basketball courts. I was hardly ever home anymore. JB lived and breathed basketball. If he wasn't at home, you knew where to find him. During organized games, he played point guard. These days, he played a lot of basketball at the park—in addition to tournaments with the Midnight Basketball League. He also watched NBA and college games on TV and played basketball video games.

JB grabbed the key to the BMW. On the way out, JB's dad stopped us, "Don't take my car out if you can't clean it. Better yet, don't take my car at all."

"I thought the BMW was your car?" I asked.

"It is my car, but my dad took it away a few months ago. He's just being a dick," he said. "Let's take your car."

On the way to the park, he asked if I'd pick up Ted. People always mistook JB and Ted for brothers. They looked a lot alike—both with beige complexions and both of them had their hair faded with curls on the top.

After I got home on a Friday, one of my girls from school called.

"Hey girl! We're going to the movies to see Titanic. Do you want to come?"

"I'm not sure. JB and I may have plans."

"Are you serious?" she said. "Okay, well you haven't chilled with us in a while. Feel free to bring him too!"

Later that evening JB and I met up with a few of my girls and a couple brought their boyfriends too to see the movie. After we left the movie, we headed back to his house. JB's dad was out of town and he was home alone.

"Hey can you pick up Ted?"

"Again?" I asked. "I thought it would be just the two of us?" But again, it was the three of us. Since JB's dad was out of town, Ted was spending the night. After an hour of Jon Madden football, I was nodding off.

"Let's play truth or dare," I suggested.

JB said, "Okay."

Ted said, "Tanisha you go first."

"I don't know…" I said. "One of you go first."

"I dare you to kiss Ted," JB said.

"What?" I asked, surprised. I was reluctant to actually do it, but Ted leaned in.

As Ted and I kissed more passionately, he slightly pressed my head his. *He's actually a good kisser*, I thought to myself. JB then put his hand up my shirt. We had a three-some that night.

The next day I came over, and Ted had already left for home. I felt a little awkward about what went on.

"You like Ted don't you?" JB asked.

"No, I don't like him."

"Why did you do what you did with him?"

"You were there too! Did you forget? I did it because you wanted me to."

"When I was with a light-skinned girl, she would have never done this," JB said.

"What? What does that mean?" I asked.

"Dark-skinned girls are just hoes. It's okay, I guess… maybe I will forgive you," JB said. I knew what he said wasn't true. I wasn't very shocked either because he was always making undercutting comments about me.

The job fair was great, and I landed a job as an office assistant for an optometrist. Dr. Weiner was the name of the doctor. He was an older man with a bald head and pointy nose. He seemed pretty nice. My work hours at the office were from 12pm-5pm. On Fridays, I picked up warm cinnamon bread, coffee, and orange juice from the bakery nearby. My coworkers were nice, except for Karen. Karen was Dr. Wiener's office manager. Karen had worked for Dr. Weiner for many years. Apparently, she was very bitter because of it. Karen wore her hair pulled back in a bun. She looked like a Mormon. She rarely smiled and was very meticulous. At the office, I had to do it her way or it wasn't right.

Amy was nice. She was one of the doctor's assistants. She taught me how to preform eye screenings with the machines. Lisa, one of the doctor's other assistants, taught me how to shape eye glass lenses, and how to fill an eyeglass prescription. I enjoyed the job. It kept me busy and the cabinets were full of free trial contact lenses.

One evening, when I got home from work, I received a phone call from JB's friend Rashid. Rashid said that JB had an accident, that he was in a lot of pain, and needed a ride to the hospital. I arrived at JB's house as quickly as I could, but by that time his dad had already arrived. JB could barely talk, but said that he was hit in the mouth while playing basketball at the park. I could tell that he was in a lot of pain. His forehead was sweating, he could barely talk, and he tapped his foot repeatedly on the floor.

I hopped in the car with JB and Mr. Barnes. The doctor did X-rays and found that JB had a fractured jaw. Luckily, it was just a hairline fracture, so the doctor didn't have to wire it shut. JB couldn't really talk, chew, or even move his mouth. He was only able to drink liquids through a straw or sip from a spoon. It took him weeks to recover and JB had lost several pounds since his accident. He questioned going back to basketball because of the injury. For now, it was best for JB not to go away to college as planned. Instead, he would wait until next year to re-apply.

A friend of mine, Meisha, also worked at the eye doctor's office. Dr. Weiner shared a suite with another doctor and Meisha was an office assistant to the other doctor. One day, as I was filing some medical charts and getting ready to leave for the day, Maya comes in to the office. I had known that Maya and Meisha were working on a science project together, but in 100 years, I never expected Maya to come into the office. I felt kinda sick to my stomach as she passed me. The last time I saw Maya was when she ran away after I slapped her.

As Maya passed through the hall she bumped me.

"Bitch!" she said as she passed.

"What?" I asked. I wasn't sure what to say or how to react.

"You heard me!" she said. I just stood there, kind of taken back. *What is she doing here?* And how could I respond to a situation like this at work? I hoped no one else saw or heard the brief encounter, but one of the employees, Lisa, did.

She walked up and asked, "Is everything okay?"

"Yes," I replied. I was almost off of work and wanted to leave as soon as possible. Maya walked to the back where Meisha was and hadn't come back since we crossed paths in the hall. It was now 5pm, and I quickly grabbed my purse, so I could make it out before Maya came back. As I was walking out, she stood next to the door.

"I called you a bitch earlier."

"Maya this is not the right time or the place," I said and walked past her. I was parked right in the front. I was just going to avoid confrontation and deal with the issue later. Maya then followed me out of the door. I didn't have electric locks on my car, so I had to put the key in the door. As I did that, Maya pushed me. When I tried to open my car door, she slapped me hard across the side of my face and head.

I had no other choice at this point but to defend myself. Lisa and Meisha quickly ran up and pulled me off of her and broke up the fight.

"We had a class project to do together. I'm so sorry. I didn't know this would happen," Meisha said.

The next day, I went into work. Karen was filing something away in the drawer. I tried to slide by.

"Excuse me! Tanisha," Karen called after me. I walked over to her and she said, "I heard about what happened yesterday, and I also heard it wasn't entirely your fault. Even though, this is a doctor's office, we cannot have that type of behavior even near the office. Good thing the doctor wasn't here when it happened. We will no longer be needing your services. We contacted Mr. Chapman already."

I enjoyed that job and felt really bad that I lost it on such terms. The next day in class, Mr. Chapman said that in order to stay in the magnet program, I had to find another job quickly. "I also suggest that you send Dr. Weiner an apology letter. I also spoke to the principle about the incident and he decided to suspend you ladies from school for one day."

"What? I'm being suspended!" I asked. He nodded, and I just walked out of Mr. Chapman's office without saying a word. I was just done. *Nothing is going right in my life!* I thought to myself. *Fuck school! Fuck Life and everything in it!*

I decided that I wasn't going back to school. It was time to make some real money. I looked in the Sunday newspaper and found an ad that said, "Wanted: Independent Sales Reps. $45-65k Starting Pay. 17 and older." This was perfect! I called the number on the advertisement and they scheduled me in for an interview. *That was easy!* I thought to myself. I went in for the interview, landed the job, and was invited back for training the next day. Quick, fast and easy! Bingo! I wasn't sure exactly what my job title was, but the guy who interviewed me said it was in direct sales, and that the pay was good. With this new job, I hoped I could afford to buy a new car and nicer clothes.

My phone started ringing startling me out of my thoughts. It was JB; maybe he was calling to apologize for his behavior the other day.

"Um…Hello?" I said.

"Can you pick me up from Ted's house?" JB asked.

"Sure, I guess…" When I got to Ted's house, JB was coming out of the house. I got out of the car to say hello. I walked up and Ted pointed to JB's neck and whispered something to him. I looked at his neck and saw a huge hickie. He ran back into Ted's house, this time coming out with a white workout towel wrapped around his neck. We walked to the car.

"I see what's on your neck," I said, confronting him right away.

"What are you talking about?"

"That hickie."

"What hickie? Danielle pitched me on the neck. She wanted you to think it was a hickie." Danielle was Ted's girlfriend. She was biracial with a beige complexion and curly hair. She lived in Oceanside and drove a mustang. She came down on the weekends and she didn't like me much. I knew this because we went on a double date once, and she said nothing to me the whole time. I didn't like the way I felt when he told me that.

"Whatever," I replied. I knew he was probably lying. Maybe, he acted this way because I wasn't light-skinned or pretty enough. Nothing was going right. Everything was falling apart. I started to think that maybe it was me. I fed into my feelings of not being good enough.

Even though I wasn't hanging out at JB's as much, I also didn't like hanging out with friends from school either. I withdrew from activities that I once liked. Hanging out with my girls was drama too. Some of my friends were upset with me because they felt that I spent too much time with my boyfriend. Who's business was it anyways? They stopped inviting me to gatherings. This hurt my feelings and caused tension between some of my closest friends.

Tunji was the only drama-free friendship I had these days. A few years back, Tunji and her family moved out of the area, but had since returned to San Jose after her mother and father separated. She was attending the high school that I refused to attend. I was glad that she was back. We started to hang out more. She was very smart and helped me with math, studying, and other school related projects.

I started training at my new job. There were about twenty other people there, of all shapes, sizes, and ages. I appeared to be the youngest person there. The training started off full of motivation. Individuals that worked there talked about how the company had changed their lives. Then, they put on a video about the history of the company and the Kirby vacuum. I began to think that I could possibly quit school and work full-time. At the end of the video, two employees slid a huge box into the front of the training room. When I saw this massive steal machine, I couldn't help but gasp. We spent the remainder of the day reviewing sales techniques. During lunch we ate sandwiches and chips and drank sodas that were catered in. Finally, at 5pm training was over. We made it and had permission to take a vacuum home for demonstrations. I was so excited! I couldn't wait to take one home to my grandparents for a demo. If anyone wanted to buy a vacuum it would be my grandparents.

When I got to the house, I couldn't wait to do the demo for Nana and Grandpa Billy. I had them sit down on the couch. Then, I put the vacuum demo tape in the VCR and played it. While I got the large box with the vacuum out of the garage, Grandpa ran to the door to give me a hand.

"Good grief! What is in this box?" Grandpa said as he helped me carry the huge box inside the house. Once the box was in the living room, it was time to assemble it. I couldn't figure out how to even get the darn thing out of the box without tearing it apart. Once again, Grandpa had to help me even though I wanted him to focus on the demo, not being my assistant. After the pieces were out of the box, I had to put the darn thing together. This time both Nana and Grandpa had to help. Finally, we figured it out about an hour later. This presentation was a total disaster. Grandpa asked the price. Like my trainer advised, I went over the benefits again. "God damn it, what is the price?!" Grandpa said. I could tell he was pretty much done with the sales part. I also remembered that after doing the demo, the product practically sells its self.

"The price is only $1,500." I told him.

Grandpa Billy flat out said, "Hell no."

I spoke to Tonia that night. She had gotten in a few fights, and she needed to focus on school in order to graduate. Her mom suggested that she finish out the year at a better school since things weren't working out for her at the school she attended.

"So, the big news is… my mom's transferring me to ST!" said Tonia. I was really excited. I thought to myself, *At last! Finally, there will be someone who knows me best, and really has my back.*

At least two weeks had gone by, and I hadn't sold any vacuums. I also had been skipping a lot of school. I was very discouraged at this point. Then, I had a vision. I thought about having to go door to door selling vacuums for the rest of my life. At that point, I decided it would be best to finish out my senior year.

I talked to Mr. Chapman and wrote the letter to Dr. Weiner apologizing for my conduct at his office. Mr. Chapman knew that I had more than enough credits to graduate early and maintained above a 3.0 grade average. He excused my absences as family related. He also set me up with an office job through a friend who owned a computer company. Now that I had another paying job, I made the decision to attend the freshmen orientation at San Jose State. For now, I would stay in San Jose, go to school and work.

A few weeks later, I met Rachael at the orientation and ran into many other familiar faces from high school. This made me again have second thoughts.

JB called and apologized for the fight between us. We made up and the next weekend his dad went out of town. JB said that he had gotten a job—an opportunity to work with a friend passing out fliers downtown to promote a new nightclub. Since his dad was out of town, he was left to watch his little sister. He asked me if I could watch her while he worked. I told him sure, that he could drop her off at my house. JB came by at about 7:30pm with his little sister, Dominique.

"Call me when you're finished!" I said as he dropped her off.

"Sure!" He said quickly and nonchalantly. He gave me a kiss on the cheek, jogged to the car, and sped off.

About thirty minutes later, I got a phone call from Tonia. Since Tonia started going to ST, we hung out all the time. Like me, Tonia was going through relationship problems with her man. Instead of hanging with our boyfriends so much, we started to hang out again with each other. It felt good to have our friendship back. I shared secrets with her and she confided in me.

"Girl! My mom just called me and said that she spotted your dude with another girl at the movie theater," Tonia announced out of the blue.

"No, it couldn't be. Maybe it was just someone who looks like him."

"Let's call my mom on three-way." After Tonia's mom confirmed that it indeed was JB, I was furious. How dare he play me like that! Having me watch his little sister while he went on a date with another girl. I called my friend Chrystal and asked if she could come over for an hour or so to watch little sis while I busted JB's ass.

As I drove to the theater, I regretted that I trusted him. I thought about all the other past lies he had told me. I arrived at the movie theater. Tonia's mom told me specifically what movie he was in. I just walked in without buying a ticket. At that point, I was so pissed I didn't care who tried to stop me. Luckily, no one noticed me walk in. I stomped to the movie that he was at. It didn't take long to spot him. He was walking into the theater with the girl. They had just got through buying popcorn. He had on his red, white, and blue Tommy Hilfiger jacket, jeans, and red and white Jordans. The same movie and outfit he wore when we went to the same movie the previous weekend. I couldn't believe the audacity. I followed them into the theater and my heart started racing. *Should I confront the girl too or just him?* I thought to myself. Now, I know it was the wrong thing to do, but I couldn't help but slap him in the head from behind. The sound echoed through the theater.

"You lied to me!" I yelled out. The theater got quiet and people were starting to stare. Tonia's mom came up from behind me.

"JB! How dare you come to the movies with another girl!" Ms. Dee yelled at JB. The girl he was with ran out of the movie theatre. He didn't know what to say. We were starting to make a scene. He got up and started walking out.

"Yeah, what are you doing JB?" I asked.

"What are you doing here?" he asked. My blood started to boil.

"You had me watch your little sister while you went out with this brizzy! I'm tired of your lies!"

"We're just friends!" he said now that the girl was gone. I told him it was over and walked out of the theater. I knew that I would have to see him again since he still needed to pick his little sister up from my house. When I got to my house, I put everything that he ever gave me, including pictures, and threw them out the door into the yard. JB arrived a few minutes later. I sent his sister to the door with her things, but he demanded to speak with me. I refused at first.

I walked to the door and shouted that I never wanted to see him again. He reached in and pulled me out of the house by my arm. "Get off of me!" I yelled, yanking my arm away.

"Listen! She's just a friend!" he yelled back. I knew he was lying and refused to listen. He grabbed my arm again.

"Don't touch me," I said snatching my arm away and pushing him back. I started walking away, but he grabbed me from behind. I turned around and socked him. He pushed me to the ground. I got up and charged after him. As I was charging him, he picked me up and slammed me to the ground, then quickly got in his car and pulled off.

Grandpa approached me one day as I left his house, "Where does your friend work?" I already knew who he was referring to.

"He doesn't," I replied.

"Is he in college?" he asked. "Nope, he's working on getting a scholarship to a college out of state." I didn't like that Grandpa was trying to intervene in my business. I felt like I was being interrogated. Needless to say, my grandfather wasn't too happy that I was dating JB.

"My 'friend' and I broke up," I said to ease his mind. Grandpa always tried to get into my business, but it was understandable. JB wasn't working or going to school and Grandpa could tell that the relationship may have had something to do with the arguments between my mom and I. Grandpa Billy was old school; he was able to put two-and-two together quickly. He saw me drive this boy around in my car, pay for the gas, and for most of our outings.

"If he's putting miles on your car, he should be changing the oil and buying the tires." Grandpa said. In his day, men had to prove their love to the lady they courted. "In my day, men were taught to be providers, I don't know what's going on with this generation. At minimum, he should have a job."

Porscha and I stayed in contact throughout the years. The next day, we meet up for lunch at the mall to catch up on things. It had been a few months since I had spoken to her. I started telling her about my boyfriend drama and big break up. Before I could finish, Porscha interrupted, "Not to cut you off, but I have some exciting news!"

"What is it?" I asked. Porscha continued to tell me about a wonderful opportunity she had gotten from her uncle John. Her uncle was a retired Dean at a historically black college. He gave Porscha a partial scholarship and opportunity to attend the college. She had already been accepted and was planning on leaving in a month. Listening as my friend continued to speak, before she could even finish her next sentence, I blurted out, "I want to go too!" I had heard about historically black colleges. I liked the movie School Daze, and I really didn't want to spend the next four years reliving the same experiences with the same people I spent the last four years with. I wanted to experience something new. Porscha seemed shocked and surprised by what I said. She said that maybe her Uncle John could enroll us both and that she would talk to him and her mother about it.

I told mom about the conversation I had with Porscha about college. I called Porscha so our moms could speak and discuss all the details. To my surprise, Mom was very supportive and thought it would be a great idea to attend the historically black college.

A few days later, Porscha, myself, and our moms were on our way to Palo Alto to meet with Porscha's uncle, Mr. Rice, at his house to discuss the details about the college.

Mr. Rice lived in a modest ranch style home, near the Stanford University Campus. When we arrived, we parked out front. Mr. Rice let us in. As we walked through the large wooden double doors, the wood floors creaked under our feet. He led us down the hall into his home office. We all sat down, and Mom and I introduced ourselves. Porscha's mom, Toni, and Uncle John quickly caught up on family members they haven't spoken to in years. Mr. Rice was a former educator before becoming Dean of the college. He was dark with a bald head and spoke with a deep voice. Mr. Rice talked about the college campus and about his experiences as a Dean for Stillman College.

"This is a Presbyterian college, so you have to behave yourselves," he warned. Uncle John also spoke highly of his daughter, Condi, her accomplishments, and her attendance at Stanford University. She now lived on the East coast and worked for the government. He said that if we did well, there may be an opportunity to transfer to Stanford or attend the graduate school there.

Once my college application was completely filled out, Mr. Rice got up to fax it into the admissions office. A few minutes later, he made a phone call into the admissions office. When he was finished with the phone conversation, he said to us, "Congratulations! You are now Stillman College students."

This was a great day. Mom seemed more excited than I was. "You know Tanisha, I'm so proud of you! I always wanted to go away to college myself, but never got the opportunity to do so. This is going to be really good for you." Mom said. I was excited too. I knew going away to college was an important move to make at the time. There were too many distractions in San Jose. Before we left, Mr. Rice said, "From now on, call me Uncle John." I smiled and thanked him for the opportunity. Uncle John made us take an oath and promise not to embarrass him.

Reflection

I knew that education was an important foundation in my life, but I didn't know how important it would become. Modeling and acting school gave me the confidence that I needed to make a new start. Plus, I got to spend time with my mom. Education would become a stepping stone and door opener to many opportunities in my life. For as long as I can remember, I've always had a strong desire to learn.

Mom was always on a budget or money was tight. I wanted a job where I made good money. I wanted to be in control of my finances, not anyone else. Early on, I learned that money was important. Even early on, emotions got in the way of some of my rational decision making.

Chapter 6

Up and Away

*E*ven at 9pm, it was very hot and humid. The inside of Porscha's grandfather house was dark, musky, and had an old smell. It kind of reminded me of my great grandma's house in Fresno. There was no air conditioning, fans, or ventilation in the house. All I could do was lay there and look out the window. This place was more country than Fresno! We couldn't even watch cable! I never had been as far South as Alabama before. Porscha's grandfather lived in Birmingham.

The atmosphere in Alabama was noticeably different than that of California. As soon I got off the plane at Birmingham-Shuttlesworth International, I instantly felt a huge difference. Even the air seemed thicker than California air. It was overcast, but it felt thick and sticky. Instead of a cold breeze, like in California, the breeze was completely void. After experiencing the humidity, I immediately began to feel like maybe going so far away for college might have not been such a good idea after all. Porscha's grandfather picked us up from the airport terminal earlier that afternoon in an old maroon Oldsmobile. He was in his eighties and drove that way down the highway. Thick forest trees lined the two-lane highway. The highways even looked different.

We finally pulled up to a small, one-story, brick country house in a small country neighborhood. The roads were paved with loose gravel and there weren't any street lights or sidewalks. The sun had set long ago, but the air was still thick and sticky. Uncle John arranged to have Mr. Bonner, Dean of academic affairs, pick us up in the morning to take us to the college campus in Tuscaloosa.

I took my cell phone out of my purse and turned on the power button. The green letters read, 'No Service'. I wished my phone worked all the way out here, but it was just for local Bay Area calls. Outside, the bugs made a low buzzing sound. I was hotter in the house than outside. So far, this trip sucked. The more I thought about it though, it wasn't just a trip. I had to actually live here. Thinking about my decision to move to Alabama, where they actually hung black people, made me start to panic. I made a decision to move somewhere I knew nothing about except lynching. I had never visited and knew nothing about Alabama. I thought we would be in Atlanta near college park. I thought to myself, *what the hell was I thinking?*

I survived the night. The next morning, Mr. Bonner pulled up to the small brick house. He drove a grayish blue sedan. Mr. Bonner had a bald head, light-brownish complexion and wore glasses. Mr. Bonner was cool; he cracked a few jokes that made us laugh. It took us about an hour to get to Tuscaloosa. On the way to the college campus, he drove us through town and pointed out where things were.

"I know since you're from Cali, you must know where the mall is located!" Mr. Bonner joked. Porscha and I laughed. He drove up to a small shopping center. The malls in California were three times this size.

"Is this the only one? I asked.

"Of course it is." said Mr. Bonner. He wasn't joking this time

Compared to California, the buildings in Tuscaloosa looked old fashioned and mostly made out of brick. The shopping mall was small, and the stores were different. The name of the grocery store in town was WinnDixie. That just sounded country. Even in town, none of the streets had sidewalks, and the street lights hung on wires. Everything in Alabama seemed old fashioned. There were no flashy cars—only old, dusty sedans.

Along the way to the campus, we stopped at Krispy Kreme Donuts and Walmart. Even the people seemed old fashion. No one wore Guess, Tommy Hilfiger or Jordans. It seemed like no one cared about their appearance. The people walked much slower and spoke with a southern drawl. In Walmart, we couldn't help but stare at the people.

Mr. Bonner must have seen the disappointment in our eyes as we left Walmart carrying our many bags. Porscha pushed the cart with the TV. So far, the only thing I was impressed with was Krispy Kreme Donuts. Mr. Bonner attempted to cheer us up by getting us excited about the many opportunities Stillman College had to offer. "There's many Greek and Non-Greek Sororities on campus," Mr. Bonner said.

We drove past a large field of luscious green vegetation. There was a sign read: 'University of Alabama'.

"We're just a few blocks from Stillman's campus," said Mr. Bonner. There were a few large brick buildings and structures, but none nearly as big as the University of Alabama's. A black steel gate with brick posts lined the campus.

We were out almost all day and the sun was starting to dim when we arrived on campus. It was a Saturday and classes didn't begin until Monday. The gravel driveway rumbled under the car tires as we pulled into the gated campus made up of several two and three story, reddish brick buildings. Some of the buildings were newer and nicer than the others.

Mr. Bonner pulled around to one of the newer buildings on campus. Mr. Bonner said, "This is the new freshman girls' dorm." We got out of the car and walked up to the building. I thought, *not too bad*. It looked like a medical suite, but with carpet. The lobby was very inviting—nice contemporary paintings on the wall. The building even had a new smell. We walked to the front desk where a girl with a clip board in front of her was sitting. Mr. Bonner explained, "I have two new residents here from California."

The girl replied, "Hi Mr. Bonner, this dorm is full and actually over capacity. You'll have to take them to Williams."

The Dean drove us back around to the front of the campus where the Williams dorm was located. The building he pulled up to was way older then the "new freshman dorm." Williams dorm was a four-story brick building that reminded me of "the projects," or at least how they showed the projects to look on television. There were many people hanging out in the front of the building. Williams was an all-girls dorm. The lobby wasn't nearly as inviting as the other dorm. The walls were made of large bricks painted off-white. No paintings hung on the wall. This building looked like a medical facility too—an insane asylum, with long, tiled hallways. The dorm had no elevators and, even though I had never been to a prison, it reminded me of a prison, but with doors.

Monday morning, before classes began, I was told that I had an appointment at the Financial Aid Office. When I got to the office, I was told to fill out a FAFSA form.

I signed student loan documents without considering the large amounts of debt I would be accumulating. I just figured that once I got my degree, I would get a good job and pay off the debt.

However, my mother read the papers. Since I was a minor and dependent, my mom signed for a parent loan. She wasn't too happy when she had to sign for a $7000 parent loan just for one semester. As I walked out of the financial aid office, there were two girls staring at me. In California, we would have considered that rude, but since I was in a different environment it was clear to me that most people from here were quite different.

"Nominee Campbell wanna be!" One of the girls said as I walked past. She said it loud enough so that I could hear. I gave both girls a wink and walked out. Tuition was just discounted, but I did not receive a full scholarship. Mom was pissed. We had both neglected to do our research. We had gotten this far. After Mom took out the parent loan, she flat out told me that I needed to get a job next school year if I wished to remain in college.. When I applied to Stillman, I also didn't research anything about the majors that were offered. I had to quickly reconsider a career as a Dermatologist when I found out that it wasn't offered at Stillman. I decided to choose International Business instead. I imagined myself as this esteemed linguist. I choose my minor to be Spanish.

Porscha and I stayed on the third floor of Williams hall. While we were lugging our luggage up the three flights of stairs, we met two girls who were from Oakland. They were also on the third floor. The two girls were cousins—Tiffany and Kendra. We started visiting each other's dorm rooms and eating with each other in the school café. It was refreshing to meet people who understood where we came from. One day, while the four of us walked to the café, there was a groups of guys standing in the square.

"Hey Cali!" One of the guys said with a country twang. After that, they all started calling us the Cali Clique. They would say, "Hey Cali!" And we all replied, "Hey!" right back.

On the college campus there were people from all over the country. I had on my white Guess jeans, a grey tank top and black sandals. My hair was down and flat ironed. The people from California dressed different, walked different, and talked different. That's why we stood out like sore thumbs. Girls were outright jealous at the attention we got from boys. We started walking past with heads high and a sultry twitch. I enjoyed the attention.

I hadn't talked to JB in days. I finally felt like I was moving on with my life. I made a promise to myself that I would make better decisions now that I was in college.

It wasn't hard to miss California. There were things that I loved doing that I could no longer do—like go to the beach, take a nice warm bath, and having privacy. Living the dorm life was definitely different than what I was used to.

Throughout my childhood, at any given time, I had to share a room with either Mom or Andre. It was different living in Williams Hall. People came from all over the country and everyone had their own way of living. Some people lived cleaner than others. Some people were just down right dirty. Porscha and I were roommates. The dorm rooms had linoleum flooring with beds on each side of the room. I placed the TV that I purchased from Walmart in the middle of my blue chest.

There was no air conditioning in Williams Hall either. The washer and dryer were located in the basement, and there was a rumor that it was haunted, so no one wanted to do laundry there at night. But, night was the only time there were any open washers. If you left your clothes in the washer overnight, there was good chance that they wouldn't be there in the morning. The bathrooms had public showers with restroom stalls. There was a bathroom on each floor of the dorm. It was rare not to find large cockroaches swimming in the shower.

Right next to Williams was the freshman guy's dorm called Jefferson. There were definitely many guys to choose from. I just wasn't that interested in any of them. None of the freshmen guys had a car or any money. Some nights it was so hot that everyone hung out in the front of the dorm building and smoked cigarettes and Black and Milds. There was a cemented quad area that was called The Square. In The Square, painted on the concrete were logos of fraternities and sororities. Some nights, fraternity and sorority members had Step battles that everyone gathered for. They would call out to their fraternity brothers or sorority sisters and do rhythmic steps.

In high school, I never played team sports, but in college I was making a new start. After my gym teacher made an announcement during class, I decided to try out for the volleyball team. He said that we could earn college credit for participating in the season. Stillman was an NCAA Division III school and pretty much anyone who was physically fit and came to practice made the team. We practiced during the week in the evenings. When there were away games, I got to skip class. In addition to skipping class and free travel for the players, we also received money for small expenses and food while on the road.

I had been in Alabama for almost two months and was finally starting to get used to it.

I had way more appreciation for small luxuries than I once had—like privacy. The showers in the dorms were far from pretty. They had clay colored tiles. In the bathrooms, were four bathroom stalls and public showers around the corner from the stalls. There were four to five showerheads and no curtains.

College wasn't much different than high school. In regards to education, the classes were not that challenging. In my math class, we were learning the same things that I learned the previous year in California. In regards to guys, the guys in the south seemed much more polite than guys in California. They ran up to open doors when a lady walked up, and always had nice compliments for the ladies that strutted by. In high school, everyone cliqued up depending on race, but now, since most of the students were black, cliques formed depending on where people were from. There were many students from Chicago, Detroit, Mississippi, as well as Alabama locals.

Mom called one evening.

"I'm about to close on the condo," she said.

"That's great mom!" I said. After I left for school, Mom decided to purchase a condominium after years of saving up.

"I have something else to tell you," she said.

"What?" I asked.

"I'm engaged!"

"To who?" I asked, shocked. I was thinking that she would say Malik.

"His name is Dave."

"Who's Dave?" I asked. Mom explained to me that she had met him at one of Andre's football games—his son played on Andre's Pop Warner team. He was one of the coaches. She said that he was really nice and she liked him a lot. After our conversation, we said our goodbyes and hung up the phone. I didn't know what to think about her big news. I had been away at college for only a couple of months and so many things were changing.

The distance between JB and I made us grow closer. When I talked to him, he said how much he missed me. I didn't give him much notice about me leaving. I started to think about was how much I missed him. Now that we were talking again, when I wasn't in class, I was on the phone with him. I would convince Porscha to walk with me to the WinnDixie to purchase calling cards. I would have to wait in line just to use the pay phone. After a few weeks of her not being able to talk to me when she wanted, Mom agreed to put a landline in my dorm room. I still had to buy long distance phone cards, but at least I got to use the phone when I wanted and could receive calls. Now, JB and I could just talk all night.

One evening, JB called. A close family member had a connection in the admissions office at Georgia Tech University and said that he may be able to get on the team there. He would live with his step mom and half brother and sister if he went. JB could stay there as long as he focused on school and red shirt the coming season for the basketball team. I had some mixed feelings, but was mostly happy and excited. I craved comfort and normality in Alabama. A few short weeks later, JB was in Atlanta and I was on the next Greyhound bus there to visit him. I arrived in Atlanta later that evening. I was so happy to see JB that I cried.

He booked a hotel room in Downtown Atlanta for just the two of us and surprised me with flowers, a cute teddy bear, and a few other souvenirs from California. I thought that was so sweet. *Maybe the time apart helped our relationship grow*, I thought to myself. We visited the underground shopping center and Lennox mall. Maybe Atlanta was where I wanted to go to school. By the end of our trip, we had no money left, but it didn't matter because we were left with fond memories.

JB and I continued to visit each other as much as we could afford to, which was every couple of weeks and talked on the phone every evening when he came home from practice. At first it was all excitement for him, but after a few weeks, I could tell that he was having a tough time in Atlanta. He was away from friends and we only saw each other once or twice a month. If he wanted to play, he would have to red shirt for a year and endure long practice schedules, drills, and studying. This lifestyle was all new for him. He also had to live with his brother and sister's mother. She had raised his twin siblings in a small suburb outside of Atlanta. She had strict household rules. Very much into education, JB's half-sister skipped a grade because she was way super smart. During school nights, there was no TV or video games—even our time on the phone was restricted.

Porscha and I flew home for winter break. JB was back in California for the holidays too.

"I'm not going back to Atlanta," he said. "I'm going to check out a school in Iowa." I didn't know what to think. I was upset, but there wasn't too much I could do about him deciding to transfer to another school. I met up with Tonia for lunch and told her how much fun Porscha and I were having away in college. Tonia was currently going to a junior college and wanted a change.

"I want to be out there with you guys!" she expressed. I called up Uncle John to let him know that I had a friend who was interested in applying to Stillman. Tonia's mom purchased her plane ticket and Tonia came to Alabama with us.

Academically, the first semester was a breeze. I had virtually no homework. It seemed like all we did was review everything we already learned in high school. Second semester, I was refocused. Economics classes were not that interesting to me. I didn't like the government and history classes either. One of my history professors spoke so slowly and looked so old that she looked like she could have been from the civil rights era. I wouldn't have been surprised if she had marched alongside Dr. Martin Luther king Jr. I couldn't help falling asleep through 80% of the class.

I had so much fun playing volleyball that second semester, I decided to try out for the softball team too. Many of our games were away since our softball field was under repair. They were rebuilding the field, so we could only use it for practice. The field was mainly dirt and fire ants. If you stood in one spot for too long, the fire ants would crawl up your legs and sting you. We traveled to Georgia, Florida, and other parts of the south to play other teams. I wasn't very good at softball. I only went up to bat a few times. We weren't the best team either. Porscha and Tonia also played on the team. After the games, we went to great places to eat—barbecue, soul food, fried fish, and hush puppies; you name it! If I had a game, my professors let me turn in assignments late.

I went out from time to time. Fraternity parties were always fun. They were usually held at the frat house or at one of the two night-clubs in town—the CC (Citizens Club) and the PC (Prime Choice).

I tried to get away from the cliquey-ness of high school, but figured out quickly that college could be like high school on a much larger scale. The sorority girls strutted about in their letterman jackets. The AKA's wore their cute pink and green jackets and the DELTA's strutted around in their bold crimson and cream. The sorority girls did their dance formations and called out their sorority calls. A girl came up to Porscha, Tonia, and I and handed us a flier for a party.

"Girl, rush week is coming up! Who wants to go with me?" Tonia asked. I kind of looked away. Porscha said, "No way am I doing that!"

"No, I'm cool," I said.

"Come on Tanisha! Pleaseeeeee!" Tonia asked. Tonia knew how to persuade me. I finally gave in and said 'yes'.

Rush week was a time where sororities and fraternities were recruiting. To be a rushee you had to go through a recruitment process, known as rush. At Stillman, they had both Greek and non-Greek sororities. The non-Greek sororities were the prerequisite to being in a Greek sorority. If you were a freshman or sophomore, and wanted to pledge, you had to start with a non-Greek sorority. During rush week, sorority recruitment was a highly structured and dressy event, with girls teetering around in the heat wearing high heels and their mother's pearls.

One afternoon, during rush week, the "California clique" was out in front of Williams chatting it up like we normally did between classes.

"I kind of like the colors for AKA," I said to my friends.

"You can't pledge AKA," Kendra said in reply.

"Why not?" I asked. I thought she was going to say something about the requirement that I had to be an upperclassman, but instead she said, "You're too dark!"

"What the hell does that mean?" I shot back in anger.

"Sorry girl, I didn't mean it like that," said Kendra. "I was told they only pledge light-skinned chicks." Now that I thought about it, most of the girls who were AKA's had pretty fair complexions.

"What?" Porscha asked surprised.

Kendra replied, "Yep, I don't know if they still do it, but back in the day, they did what was called a paper bag test."

"What the hell is that?" I asked more confused than ever. Kendra ran and got a paper bag.

"If your skin is darker than this bag, they won't pledge you," She explained. That was the dumbest thing I had ever heard. I rolled my eyes as the girls started to compare skin tones. If skin tone was a requirement to get into their sisterhood, I was no longer interested. From that day forward, if I did pledge, I would pledge DELTA.

In the college cafeteria, we ate lunch, dinner, and breakfast if we got up early enough. Breakfast usually consisted of grits, eggs, toast, sausage, and biscuits. At first, the food was good, but as time went on, I realized that the many selections in the café got very old, very fast. The food was bland, and I quickly found out that they served the same thing day in and day out. The café was only open at certain times of the day for limited hours.

Since the age of fifteen, I had been working and earning my own way. This was the first time in three years that I hadn't had a job and my own spending money. I also missed not having my car. When I purchased calling cards to make long distance calls, I would call into the 1-800 on the back of the card and say that my phone call was cut short to get free minutes added. Auntie Vanessa worked for a large corporation and found a way to connect me long distance without her being on the phone. During her work hours, when she was available, she would connect me to people long distance. Purchasing toiletries, food, and entertainment all added up quickly. Before the end of the month, the money that my family had sent was gone. College life was a hard life.

Freshman year, Porscha, Tonia, and I made a pact with each other that when one of us did get money, we would look out for one another. If one of us, went out we all went out. When one of us had money we treated one another to a meal or paid for one another to get into nightclubs if we had it. Maybe it was the pact that made me decide to go through with rush week with Tonia.

That evening, there was a secret meeting for the girls who were interested in pledging with the non-Greek sorority. It was located in the meeting room of the sophomore dorm. At the meeting, they discussed the requirements for being in the sorority. A girl stood up and talked about sisterhood and what the sorority represented—about how it was required that we attend socials and mixers.

She said, "Sisters are also required to participate in philanthropic activities." There was a certain time commitment to maintaining an active membership in the group, which I knew I didn't really want to commit to. Another member passed out a calendar of upcoming events for rush week that we had to attend if we wanted to pledge. I looked on the calendar—spring break was coming up the next week. I had plans of going home for the break.

I spent a lot of time in the dorms, but not by choice. At least half of the students who attended Stillman were residents of the south. On weekends and holidays, most students went back home. In Tuscaloosa, places didn't stay open very late and many stores and restaurants were closed on Sundays. Tuscaloosa was considered a college town and most businesses catered to the college community. On nationally observed holidays, the town seemed empty. To get away sometimes, on the weekends, we went home with a friend that we met on campus. She had a car and was from Birmingham. On some weekends, we bummed a ride to Birmingham with her.

We did have some entertainment on the college campus. There were concerts, football games, and step shows on our small college campus. Since there wasn't much to do, my friends and I started venturing out a little. We hung out at the University of Alabama campus. A friend of ours, who we met at one of our campus concerts, worked for one of the number one radio stations in Birmingham. His radio name was Bartel Bartel.

I started to meet new people at school and from traveling outside of Tuscaloosa. In Birmingham, we visited the radio station. Some weekends, he even let us stay at his apartment. From his place, we caught a cab to the mall. We went to step shows in Birmingham and met people from all over. The guys in the south loved California girls. We got a lot of attention because we were different.

At 2am, I was woken up out of a deep sleep. It was Tonia. "What is going?" I asked very confused.

"We have a meeting! Didn't you read the calendar!" Tonia exclaimed. I thought the calendar said 2pm.

"What? I'm not going!" I said.

"Come on hurry up!"

"I need to get dressed."

"Bitch! Look at what I have on." She wore a pair of grey sweats and a tank top. I had on a long white night shirt. I slipped on some jeans and sneakers under my long white t-shirt and headed out the door—probably with sleep still in my eyes.

The "meeting" was being held in the music hall. There were about fifteen others freshmen girls there besides Tonia and I. We all had on lounge clothes. After a minute or so of gathering, a girl said, "Pledges! Get in line!" I just stood there. "Get the fuck in line!" Shouted the girl. We all hurried into a line. In my head I thought, *Are you serious?* I knew this was probably just part of one of their rituals.

As we stood in line, the girl announced that we were chosen to pledge, and to prove our loyalty, we would have to undergo a series of tests. *Umm…I don't know about all of that!* I thought. A girl with light brown skin and short hair like Toni Braxton came down the row, looking at each girl.

"You'll need to change your hair!" She said to one girl standing in line. "How cute, you have on slippers. This is not a fucking living room!" Both girls stood quietly. Then, she came up to me. "What the fuck do you have on?!" I recognized this girl from one of my classes. I had a sense that she didn't like me. *Now here's her chance to belittle me. Great!* I didn't say a thing. "What the fuck do you have on bitch? Is that a night gown? You think you're all that huh bitch? You ain't shit." She was actually starting to get to me, but before I could get upset she moved onto the next victim.

The next morning, I walked to class tired as hell. I thought about how I would never attend another "meeting." I thought to myself, *From now on, Tonia is on her own.* As soon as I finished my thought, a white truck with a large confederate flag flying in the air sped by. "Niggers!" The guy in the passenger seat yelled out. If I had happened to forget where I was, I quickly remembered at that point.

In town, there were white sides of town and black sides. There were black ghettos and black upscale-middle class neighborhoods. If black and white people in Tuscaloosa coexisted, they never really communicated.

Tonia was disappointed that I had decided I was not staying to pledge. Tonia tried to convince me, but I wasn't going to any more early morning meetings just to eventually wear a jacket with a logo and go to parties.

My freshmen year in college quickly passed. By springtime, JB was back home for good. Things didn't work out for him in Iowa, and he decided to come back to San Jose. Before the end of the school year, JB was back home. I was now back in California for the summer. I wasn't sure if I wanted to go back to Stillman College for my sophomore year, but I didn't have an alternative school yet. Mom was preparing for her wedding. I really wasn't too into Mom getting married. I had met Dave, and he seemed nice, but I didn't know him. He had a few children from a previous marriage. Dave's son and my brother Andre were the same age; they got along well.

That summer, I submitted job applications and quickly landed a part-time job at the mall in a popular lingerie store. To my surprise, I also landed a temp job as a receptionist during the day at a biopharmaceutical company.

Once again, J.B. and I quickly revamped our relationship. After work, I started visiting him. Until one day, while I was over at his house hanging out, there was a knock at the front door. Everyone was gone, and he wasn't expecting anyone. He quickly got up and peeked through the curtain to see who it could be. I just assumed it was one of his boys coming by, wanting to shoot some hoops like always. As soon as JB peered through the window, he jumped back not realizing that I was now standing right behind him.

"Who is it?" I asked, now very curious as to why he was so jumpy. By his reaction, I automatically knew something was up. I needed to see who was behind that door. I walked to the door and opened it. JB quickly flung himself in front of me. When I opened the door, I got a quick glimpse of a girl. She was tall, light-skinned with a short bob haircut.

"So it's like that JB!" the girl yelled as the door slammed shut.

"Let her in!" I yelled, but JB made me promise to stay in the house until she left. After about five minutes, the girl went back to her car and pulled off. About a minute or two later, I left. I knew she was going to come back to the house since she was crazy enough to show up unexpectedly. So, I circled the neighborhood. Bingo! As soon as I pulled back around, there she was. I flagged her down, as she drove past.

"Excuse me! Can I please talk to you?"

"Who are you?" she asked, visibly upset. We met later that evening at Denny's and she gave me the low down on JB. JB had been seeing her for six months. I was pissed, but not surprised. I decided not to mention the meeting to JB.

After the meeting with the girl she starting calling me, and we actually started hanging out. We went to the mall, the movies, and I even hung out at her house. She lived in a large house located in the East Hills. Her parents were educators. I knew I was tripping when I was at her house one day, sitting on her day bed. While looking in her mirrored closet doors she said, "When JB and I had sex, he used to look at himself in the mirror like he was doing something." I wanted to slap her, but I didn't. I just told her I had to leave.

What started off as a productive summer, ended up being a crazy love triangle. We were both seeing JB. As things progressed, though, we both started to become fed up with his lies. So one night, the girl and I partnered up and ambushed him at his mother's house with eggs and toilet paper. But, he got us back and shot at us with his Beebe gun. Also, his mother was home and came outside to the chaos at 10pm. She threatened to call the cops.

"Aren't you away at college Tanisha?" His mom asked. I was so embarrassed.

After that night, I decided it was best to go back to Tuscaloosa to finish out my sophomore year.

Coming back to Stillman was bittersweet. Some of the friends I made my freshman year either dropped out or transferred to a school near home. Tiffany and Kendra, the two cousins that I met, moved back to California. Tonia and Porscha were both in Tuscaloosa. Tonia was living on campus in the dorms, and Porscha had found an off campus apartment. Mom said that she couldn't afford to send me money. So, I saved the money I earned from my summer job. Life started to get real, real quick. Completing college proved to be tougher than I had imagined. I had accumulated a lot of student debt. This year, to cut down on college tuition, Mom and I decided it was best to stay off campus. Now that Mom was a homeowner, she could no longer afford to help me pay for my expenses; that meant I had to find a job.

I had made enough money over the summer to get my car shipped and had a little left over to get me through the month. I found an apartment near the University of Alabama. They were university apartments and based on a questionnaire, they placed me with three roommates. Two of my roommates went to UA, and the other one went to Stillman. We each had our own rooms and shared two bathrooms.

This time, Mom flew down to Tuscaloosa with me and stayed for a week to help me move into my apartment. It was nice for her to be able to experience the college life with me. My car hadn't arrived yet, so Mom rented a car. We went shopping, out to eat, and site seeing. I really enjoyed Mom's company. When it was time for her to go, I gave my roommate, Faith, twenty dollars to drop Mom off at the Birmingham Airport.

As soon as Mom left for California, I started my job search. I found a job as a food server at one of the largest restaurants in Tuscaloosa. The restaurant offered a casual family dining experience. Many of the people who worked there were students at the University of Alabama. I was the only student who worked there that attended Stillman.

Classes started, and I was now working, but something didn't feel right. I was starting to feel sluggish and tired all the time. Since I worked at the restaurant, the smell of the food started to get to me. I had no appetite. I knew something was up. One time, while at work, a customer ordered the prime rib rare. When I brought the plate to the table, the customer started to pour globs of ketchup all over the meat. I quickly excused myself and ran to the restroom to vomit. My breasts were very sore. That night I went to the drug store after work. I didn't wait until I got home. As soon as I purchased the pregnancy test, I took it into the drug store bathroom. In the public stall, I quickly read the directions and peed on the stick. The first pink line appeared, then there was a second slight pink line. The test read positive. I couldn't believe it. I had used condoms most of the time and had been on and off of birth control throughout the years. Up until this point, I had never thought I could get pregnant.

I was going to be a mother. When I told Porscha and Tonia, my girls looked at me like I was crazy.

"Are you going to keep it?" asked Tonia. Until then, I hadn't thought about what I was going to do. I told JB and, of course, he wasn't happy about the idea of me choosing the have a baby. I was very conflicted. I continued going to school and working—being stubborn.

I fought with the idea of abortion for weeks. I didn't have much time. Mom suggested that I do what was best for me, but just think clearly about the implications of both.

Mom purchased me a plane ticket so that I could see a doctor in California. My OB/GYN told me about the abortion methods and also adoption. Neither of those seemed like a viable option.

It was a Saturday, I had a day off of school and I didn't have to work until that evening. I needed rest more than anything. My phone rang. I had caller ID so I checked before answering. The call was from a 510 number, which is the Bay Area, so I picked up. It was JB's mother.

"Hello," I said.

It was JB's mother. We talked very briefly, but ultimately she said, "You shouldn't have this baby. You both have your lives ahead of you." She was a nurse, and she attempted to convince be that abortion was the best option. I felt backed into a corner. I felt like it was the logical thing to do, but not the right thing to do.

"Okay, I'm going to get it done." While my heart shouted, *No!* I talked to Mom, and she found an abortion clinic at a hospital in Atlanta. I was very bitter that JB wasn't any part of this traumatic experience.

Mom helped me arrange the appointment with the hospital. Two nights later, I drove to Atlanta with three of my friends. My appointment was first thing in the morning and Atlanta was a two-hour drive. I decided it would be best to leave that night for my appointment, so we could be back for class late morning. All I could afford was fifty dollars a night for a hotel. We arrived and the sign read: "Vacancy $39.99." That was prefect. I could also now afford a tank of gas to get back home. The room was down the stairs of what looked like a basement cellar. The hallway was dimly lit with only a red light to illuminate it. This was why the front desk guy called it 'the dungeon'. I thought he was joking. The room light in the dungeon was not much better.

Reflection

By the grace of God, I made it to college! From the beginning, I knew I was going to college—not going wasn't an option. My experience at Stillman was very interesting. My experience there was filled with exciting times as I explored life. I wanted freedom to explore under my own terms, and that's why I chose to go away to college. I also wanted to make my mother proud of me.

I had much desire to experience a life different from that of my mother and grandmother. My mother told me about so many missed opportunities that she wished she would have taken. She wished that she had the opportunity to go away for college, but couldn't because she was a teen mother. That's why I learned to take opportunities as they came to me.

Chapter 7

Going Back to Cali

The morning sickness was gone, but I felt empty and weak. Now, I felt even more lonely and extremely home sick. Outside, snow lightly covered the ground. Snow days usually excited me, but not today. I looked into the bathroom mirror and cried, criticizing my pathetic reflection. I had class that evening and needed to get dressed. In class, I was like a zombie—a blank expression on my face, just staring into space. During our break, I told my professor I wasn't feeling well and she excused me to the campus nurse. I walked out of class and, instead of going to the nurse, I took a detour and found myself in the campus chapel. I dropped to my knees and sobbed, asking God for forgiveness. Shortly after, a lady came out of the temple. She helped me up from my knees and hugged me until I stopped crying.

"Sweetheart, are you okay? Do you want someone to talk to?" I was eventually able to gather the words and said, "No thanks, I'll be fine. Thank you." I walked out without saying another word.

For weeks, I pretty much stayed to myself. I went to class, worked, and came home. The first semester of my sophomore year had concluded. I was now heading back to California for winter break. Once I had arrived, I felt joyful and relieved to be with family. I had dinner over Nana and Grandpa's house. Mom and I went Christmas shopping, and I got to spend time with my grandparents. I even spent some time with JB. We weren't back together, but eventually one thing led to another. Before I left JB's house, Mr. Barnes was working on his Porsche 911 race car in the garage.

"Hey Tanisha, come here for a second," he called out. "So, how's school?"

"It's good! I'm just a little home sick and ready to come back to California."

"Well you may want to leave that chump alone," he said, referring to his son. "There's no future there. Could you imagine my son playing video games all day while you worked to maintain the household?" I shook my head 'no' as he continued, "You have your whole life ahead of you. I think you should finish college. There are many young men that are doing things with their lives. My son is not doing anything for himself." I didn't really respond back to Mr. Barnes, but I heard what he said. It was the same thing everyone else told me— that I needed to move on. I wasn't sure if I was ready to move on.

When my trip to California was over, I was a bit disappointed. I was really ready for a change. Going to Stillman had been a great experience, but I was so ready for something new. For the next couple of weeks after I'd returned, I maintained my normal schedule: school, work, and television. One day, I woke up feeling extremely weak and nauseous. I started to have the same symptoms I had just a few weeks prior. I recalled how J.B. and I slept together without protection. I felt like, I may be pregnant. That night, I went to the drug store and took a pregnancy test. The test read positive.

I found myself relieved and excited at first. Ever since I had the abortion, I had been very depressed. I thought, *Maybe I was meant to be a mother*. Then, my reality hit. I thought about being back at square one. I was in college two thousand miles away from my family. Then, like a river, a slew of worries washed over me. I worried about how JB would react to the news about being pregnant again. I told Porscha immediately and, that night, I planned to tell you-know-who. After telling Porscha the news, I called J.B.

"Hey what's up," I said.

"What's up?" he replied.

"Do you have a second to talk?" I asked.

"Uh, well I was about to go play ball with Damien."

"Well, this is kind of important."

"Okay, what is it?"

"I just took a pregnancy test, and it was positive," I said. JB didn't really have a response; he just said that he would call me back later, but he never ended up calling.

The next evening, my phone rang and it was a call from a 510 area code that I didn't recognize. I knew that it was a Bay Area area code, so I picked up. On the other end of the phone was JB's mom. I thought that she may have been calling to call a truce since JB probably told her that I was pregnant again, or maybe she was calling to have a heart-to-heart conversation. Instead, she started to yell at me through the phone—telling me that her son had his whole life in front of him and that we were too young and immature for a child. After she had calmed down, she then attempted to convince me to terminate the pregnancy. She accused me of using her son. I couldn't breathe or find the words to say back to her. She convinced me the first time to have an abortion, and a second one was not an option.

After the conversation between JB's mother and I, I calmed down and decided to give J.B. a call. The phone rang once. JB answered, and then immediately his put his friend Damien on the phone. "How's your friend out there?" I asked.

"You know, JB is JB."

"Is he really looking for a job?"

"Not really. When we hang out we usually play Madden or NBA hoops or hoop at the park."

"Is he being good?"

"Ha-ha! What does that mean?" That was confirmation that he was seeing other people..

At least three weeks had gone by since I had spoken to JB. I had to still focus on school and Economics was my hardest class. My economics Professor was from Kenya and spoke with a deep accent. Economics was a difficult class and the accent made it even harder to understand. It was in this class that I met Cliff, a senior who majored in accounting. He seemed to grasp the concepts being taught. I sat next to him in class most of the time. He was tall, with a caramel complexion and played basketball for the Stillman team. He helped me translate what the professor was teaching.

Midterms were coming up and one day after class Cliff asked, "Do you want to study?"

"Sure!" I said. As far as I was concerned, Cliff was the finest guy at Stillman. He drove a nice car, a job, and he was about to graduate. My roommates were out for the evening. I tidied up my apartment and bedroom. I wore some cut off jean shorts, a pink tank top, my hair pulled back into a pony tail, and a couple spritzes of my favorite perfume. I wanted to go for the sexy lounge-around-the-house look.

"You look nice," he complimented.

"Thanks," I said with a smile. "Come in, have a seat. Do you want anything to drink?" Within twenety minutes we had dropped the book and were making out. A relationship sparked between us. We studied together and for the first time in years, I didn't think about JB. To make JB jealous, I even told him I was seeing someone.

Cliff came over to hang out often. The last night he came over, we had sex. There was so much passion between us during, but afterwards blood started coming out of me. It was more than a usual period—dark red ran down my legs. Cliff rushed me to the emergency room, and I cried all the way there. I thought I was losing my baby. When I arrived in the emergency room, it was late so they were able to see me right away. Concerned, Cliff followed behind. They put me in a room and the doctor started doing some tests. I asked Cliff if he could step out for a moment while I talked to the doctor. I told the doctor that I was pregnant. I then had Cliff come back into the room.

"What is going on?" Cliff asked me, concerned.

I took a deep breath then told him, "I'm pregnant!" Cliff's eyes got huge.

"Not from you. From my boyfriend in Cali," I said. I had mentioned him to Cliff once or twice before.

"Oh I see. I have to tell you something too. I have a baby on the way. My girlfriend's pregnant and we're supposed to get married this summer," He confessed. Now my eyes got big.

Luckily, my baby was alright. After that night, Cliff and I stopped studying together. We said 'hello' in passing, and I stopped sitting next to him in class. Before finals were over, I started packing my room in my apartment. After I took my last final, I was ready to get on the road. I was ready to go home. Packed down, I drove across the country to California.

Now that I was back in California, I was relieved. I had more options to choose from in regards to my future. I was gone for just about two years, and it seemed like many things had changed. There were new highways built leading downtown. The skating rink that I once frequented with my friends on Friday nights became a furniture store. Rent was on the rise and, in order to get my own place, I had to find a good paying job. It was also a good idea to enroll in another college. Now that I was having a baby, in my eyes, finishing college was more important than ever. I was following my mother's advice. "Don't take any time off," Mom said. "Just keep going; once you stop, it will be harder to go back."

Luckily, I maintained good grades at Stillman and, after applying to Cal State East bay, I was accepted. This was the first and only school I applied to transfer to. Most of my units from Stillman College transferred over. They had flexible classes offered in the evening. I was able to work during the day and take classes in the evening. I decided to change my major to Human Development. I was having a child, so a job with heavy traveling or moving overseas no longer seemed like a viable option. My new major was a cross between Sociology and Anthropology. It was geared toward careers which served the public— like social work, counseling, non-profit, and education.

In all honesty, I just wanted to be done with college. After the emergency scare with Cliff, I found an OB/GYN near the college campus. A few days before midterms ended I found out I was having a boy. I was so excited and couldn't wait to be able to hold him! I also passed economics class with a B. Things were looking up. I had so much hope for the future and a strong desire to provide for my son and myself. I felt like I had to find a full time job. I decided that, even though I was pregnant, I was going to start looking for a job now. I went to an employment agency, and it only took a few days to find a job as an Office Assistant. The job was with a small family-owned business. It was a printing firm and publishing company. The owners were a young married couple; a Japanese guy and his wife. His wife was a white lady and they had four young children.

Before I began interviewing for jobs, I knew it would be a good idea not to mention that I was pregnant. I was going on five months, but I wasn't really showing yet. When I wore a tight shirt, it just looked like I had a little gut. Although, I had started wearing looser clothes since Mom took me shopping for maternity clothes. Most of my clothes were tight and no longer fit me. I had to wear my jeans un-buttoned and unzipped with a long shirt.

I hadn't announced my pregnancy to my extended family yet. As of now, only a few people knew—including my mom, JB, and a few of my close friends. I had Mom promise not to tell the rest of the fam-ily. She said that she would leave it up to me to tell them when I was ready. The last person I wanted to tell was Grandpa. I felt like he would be the most disappointed out of anyone. I really didn't want to disappoint him.

I spent a lot time working, planning, and anticipating the future. In my eyes, life would start again once the baby was born. I was excit-ed to see just how everything would unfold. My grandfather finally found out I was pregnant. He ended up finding out from someone else before I was ready to tell him. He confirmed the news with me one day.

"So I heard you're having a baby. Is it true?" Grandpa asked.

"Yes Grandpa," I said in a quiet, somewhat ashamed voice. He could hardly look at me.

Some days were worse than others. Grandpa barely spoke to me during the pregnancy. Since Grandpa knew, everyone else in the family found out. I got some criticism from family members who felt like I was making a bad decision. Some people had the need to share their pessimistic views on what they thought the outcome of my situation would be like. I felt disappointed in myself because I had disappointed my family by not finishing school or getting married first.

"You're going to lose your pretty little figure," someone told me. Everyone close to me was concerned and had suggestions.

"You should just move on and let him be," my friends and family said. I had done just that, but remained hopeful that maybe he would decide to come around after the baby was born. JB and I weren't talking, so I had to get information about him through trusted sources. I had heard from a friend of a friend that JB was seeing another girl. According to his little sister, him and this girl were pretty serious. Even though I felt like he was a jerk, I did miss our friendship. I felt this weird connection with him now that I was pregnant with his child.

Enough was enough, and I decided to go to his home to confront him.

"She's just a friend!" he claimed. Now, I knew when he way lying.

"How can you date someone else knowing you have a child on the way?"

"I'm not sure if it's even mine. You were fucking Cliff around the same time."

"I didn't start seeing him until after I knew I was pregnant!"

"Even better!" JB walked outside and his phone rang, so I picked up. There was his girlfriend on the other line. She said that she was his girlfriend. She said that she knew I was pregnant, but the baby wasn't his. At this time, JB came in and intercepted the call. He told me to get the fuck out of his house. It was easy for him to move on because he wasn't the pregnant one.

"That's not my baby! It's your boyfriend Cliff's!" JB denied that he was the father of our child. I left the house in a rage. I was very upset. The stress of it all was barreling down on me. I was now twenty-eight weeks pregnant. I had gained a lot weight during the pregnancy. At my prenatal appointment, the doctor told me that I had developed high blood pressure. He hooked me up to heart monitors and asked, "Can you feel that?"

"Yes, I've been feeling that squeezing sensation for a few days," I told him.

"That is a contraction; you are having pre-term labor. We'll need to monitor the baby and do additional tests." I had to be hospitalized. After two days, I was released from the hospital and put on observation. The doctor suggested bed rest.

Family and friends came to visit me in the hospital. JB even came to the hospital. We didn't talk much about the situation that transpired a few days prior. I felt a slight glimmer of hope that maybe he was coming along.

Twelve weeks later, I gave birth to a healthy baby boy, Cameron. The way that I felt about my son, was a love that is completely indescribable. Above anything and all things in my life, he came first. I decided that, despite me being a young mother, I was not going to think of myself as a statistic. I knew that having this baby was the best decision for me. I started to see life differently. It wasn't just about me anymore. I wanted my son to have a father, but I didn't have time to chase him around. I was more than ever determined to finish college and become successful.

Being told that I couldn't do something, just gave me the drive to go above and beyond. I went back to work at the printing press. The price of diapers and formula alone was killing my pocket book. I wasn't making much money—barely making ends meet. I knew that if I continued to work there, I would never be able to afford to move out on my own.

In my free time, I applied to jobs. Finally, I got a call back about a front office position at a tech firm. I went to the first interview, and they invited me back for a second interview the next day. During the second interview, I was hired permanently. I was so happy! I started working at the front desk of the large tech company. I was making more money and now had health benefits.

Reflection

When life gives you lemons, make lemonade! My son gave me the momentum that I needed to make things happen in my life. So many people told me about what I couldn't do, and I used their doubts in my favor as energy to prove all of the naysayers wrong.

Chapter 8

Pimps and Prostitutes

Tonia and I decided to become roommates. We found an apartment across town. Tonia's uncle was subleasing his two-bedroom apartment. Rent was affordable and close to work.

We didn't consider much about moving, besides wanting our own place. Parking at our new apartment was terrible. I had a new baby and had many things to carry from my apartment to the car—diaper bag, backpack, purse, stroller and sometimes groceries. The first week I was there, I double parked in the front of the apartment to drop off groceries. When I came back out, my car as gone. It had been towed.

I also commuted back and forth from the East Bay during the week for school. Traffic was terrible and it took me over an hour to get to school in the evenings. In class, I could hardly keep my eyes open.

The professor said, "Today, we are looking into Piaget's theory." *Another boring evening*, I thought to myself. The professor went on lecturing, "Childhood is the age span ranging from birth to adolescence. According to Piaget's theory of cognitive development, childhood consists of two stages: pre-operational stage and concrete operational stage."

Even though I was tired, I enjoyed the lectures. They were quite interesting actually. Psychology helped me see the world differently. I was interested in how the mind worked. This lecture made me think about the past and the experiences I had as a child. Learning about how the mind worked, helped me cope with being a single parent. I also kept my love for arts and entertainment and took a theatrical makeup class.

As roommates, Tonia and I started to argue about everything from who gets the parking spaces, to having guests over, to doing the dishes. Our priorities were completely different. I had a new baby, work, school, and a conflicting schedule. Being roommates was starting to put a strain on our friendship.

I arranged child care at a center near work. JB's father and my mother rotated picking the baby up from childcare so that I could attend college. I was also the sole provider for our son. I had no help financially with childcare, even though most of my paycheck went towards that, beside day-to-day necessities. I was starting to get fed up.

I had a busy day at work. There was an accident on the freeway on my way to school, and I was late to class. I parked and ran into the building. Once I got inside, I forgot where I was going. *What class do I have tonight?* I looked, and I was on the wrong floor. The room started to spin. My breathing became labored, my heart was pounding, and I started to get hot. I was having a panic attack. I sat on a chair in the hall outside one of the classrooms. I couldn't do anything but hold my head between my legs. I sat for about five minutes while gathering my breath and thoughts. Once my mind stopped racing, I found the nearest restroom. I went to the sink and splashed some water on my face. I recalled what day it was and this helped me remember which class I needed to go to. I hurried off to class.

I enjoyed my new job as a receptionist for the tech company. I sat in a large lobby and answered the switch board. I wore a head set and had to dress up in blouses and cute little skirts and dresses. Only on Fridays were we allowed to dress casually. My boss, Jim, was the Director of Human resources and lived on the East Coast. He was only there for a week or so throughout the month. This was a very large corporation, and they had locations all over the world. I got to meet and greet people that flew in from many different places. Business men would fly in monthly to attend board meetings. Anyone who entered the large building had to check in with me. One board member, named Manny, would stand at the front desk when he came in for meetings and chat with me for a while. He was white, handsome, with short greying hair, and in his forties. I knew he was married because he wore a wedding ring.

When Jim was on the East Coast, and there weren't any meetings, it was generally slower. During the slower times, I took the opportunity to complete homework. At times, work got very boring. After finishing my homework, it was only me, a phone, and the computer. I read and researched things online for school.

This was when I discovered social networks. Having a baby, working, and going to school, I hardly had time to go out or socialize. The use of social media exposed me to a new world. At work, I chatted with people from the same area. I wasn't old enough to get into cool nightclubs like some people I knew. Many of my friends had turned twenty-one already or went out using their older sibling's IDs.

Beth and I still talked often; she and I had stayed in contact over the years. When I moved back to California, I found out that Beth had a baby girl. Our children were about the same age. Beth and I met up for lunch from time to time. Beth had an office job and she also had a social media page.

I decided that I would create a page too. I didn't want to use my real name for my page, so I made up an alias. I also uploaded a popular chat program to my computer at work. I uploaded the chat program because my boss thought it would be an easier way for the department to communicate. I thought it would be interesting to chat with friends and other people instantly. On my social media page, I was feeling a little curious, so put my sexuality as bisexual. A guy, who was an engineer from San Francisco, started to hit me up. I gave him my chat handle, and we started chatting often.

I began to focus more energy on getting back into my pre-pregnancy clothes. I exercised on the weekends and during my lunch hour. After I lost the baby weight a few weeks later, I posted a new picture on my profile.

I started to get a lot of direct messages from random people. One message was from a girl named Toya. I was excited to read her message, but bummed to see that there weren't any pictures on her profile. I gave her my chat handle anyway.

I continued to work and attend college in the evenings. I lived with family for a while, so that I could afford a place of my own. I was able to eventually find an apartment.

It was Monday, and there was another board meeting. Executives from all over the country, and some from other countries, flew in for the meeting. Manny came in and stopped by my desk to talk.

"Hey, do you have an email address or chat?" he asked.

"Sure," I said, not really thinking about it. I wrote down my email and chat handle on a yellow sticky note and handed it to him.

I felt like I made decent money until I moved out on my own. It wasn't easy supporting a child by myself. Rent, childcare, food, bills, diapers, formula, and gas to go to and from school all added up quick. My checks didn't really go a long way. I had no furniture for my new place.

I decided to meet up with that girl Toya that I met through the social network. We exchanged numbers and after talking on the phone we decided to meet up. I got to her house later that evening. When I pulled up, I sat in my car for a few moments. Then, I got up the courage to get out of the car and walk up to the door. I tried to dress casual like I was going to the mall. I had on a cute shirt, jean skirt, and some flats. I walked up to the modest one story house; it was near the high school Tonia attended before transferring to ST. A girl with brown skin, like mine, and long black hair answered the door. She was cute, but looked a lot like me. A few of her younger siblings were at home. We went to her room and sat down.

"Don't mind them!" she said, talking about her little brothers who ran up and down the hallway. We made small talk in her room. She mentioned that she was the only girl and the oldest.

"You are much prettier in person," she said.

"Thanks! You're pretty too!" I replied.

"So what are we going to do?" she asked me.

"I'm not sure," I said, kind of confused by what she was asking. She turned towards me and kissed me on the lips. Then, one thing led to another. She lifted up my skirt and went down on me.

When I left, I decided not to tell anyone about what had just happened. I felt conflicted. Did this mean I was gay?

At work the next day, I logged onto chat. My engineer friend from San Francisco sent me a message while I was away from my desk.

"How much would you charge to be with you?" he asked. *That was a very random question*, I thought. I was down to my last forty dollars and didn't get paid until next week. I was going to ask my mom to borrow money, but I still owed her from last time. Unsure of how to respond to the direct question, I just sent a message that said, "$300". He sent a message back that said, "Okay. When?" I replied, "Tonight."

I dressed up like I was going out to a nightclub. I wore a gold one-strap halter-top that I purchased for my birthday and tight, dark blue denim jeans with stiletto heels. I pulled up to a loft building in San Francisco. I couldn't believe that I dressed up and drove all the way to San Francisco to meet with a complete stranger for sex.

After I found parking on the street, I called him as he requested. He buzzed me into the side gate. A young white guy in his late twenties, average height and weight, but not an athletic body, came to greet me. He looked like he had premature balding, but I gave him a hug and was thankful that he looked normal. Inside his place, he had large windows on one side of the loft apartment that over looked the busy city intersection. When I looked out the window, I could see my car parked on the street. His place was decorated nicely; it was neat, clean, and contemporary. I followed him up the stairs to his bedroom in the loft. Before I sat down, I looked around. He asked if he could video tape it.

"I guess," I said, a little hesitant. He took out the tripod and plugged the digital camera into the television. The image of myself sitting on the bed glared back at me. He handed me three one hundred dollar bills. Then, we started. Afterwards, I thought it wasn't that bad.

I got an email from Manny. "I just wanted to say hello. I'm flying my private plane to Lake Tahoe would you like to join me?" One thing my mother taught me was to never fool around with a married man, so I kindly declined. "I'm moving into my new place this weekend. I'll have to decline this time," I responded.

Manny typed back. "I will be out there next week. How about we meet at the coffee shop?" Manny was a very sweet guy, but I wasn't into him like that. But I thought, *Hey why not. I would love a free cup of coffee.* I replied, "Sure, why not!"

When Manny came to San Jose, I met with him at the coffee shop. He handed me an envelope full of one hundred dollar bills.

"What's this for?" I asked him.

"Your new place." There was ten, one hundred dollar bills in the envelope.

"Thank you, but you didn't have to do this!" I replied. The rational part of me wanted to hand the money back, but the irrational part of me spoke louder and told me to keep it. So, I put the envelope in my purse and continued to sip my iced chai latte.

"You owe me one," Manny said with a wink. I didn't know what that meant.

"Okay," I said. I now had enough money to purchase some furniture for my new apartment.

A few days later, my engineer friend sent me a direct message. I decided to take him up on his offer for a second date. This time I wore a white lacy dress with pink roses along the strap. I had started to think about the implications of what I was doing. I didn't like him, and he only liked my body. We knew nothing about one another. To tell the truth, I really didn't want him to know anything about me. It was something that I did for money. After I left, I decided that was going to be the last time I saw him. I stopped responding to his direct messages and texts; he quickly got the idea.

Through the social network, I had gotten a direct message from a photographer in my area. He asked if I would be interested in a test shoot for magazine and online modeling. He asked, " would do the shoot for Time for Print or TFP?" I didn't know what that meant. After I asked, the photographer explained to me that a TFP is when a model shoots with a photographer in lieu of pictures for their portfolio and the photographer owns the rights to the photos to do what they pleased with the images.. He said that he managed a few models and could get me other paid gigs.

On the weekend, I met up with the photographer for the test shoot. I pulled up to the large ranch style home in Saratoga. His name was Rich. He was a white guy in his early fifties. He seemed a little strange, but from my past experience with photographers, I knew them to be a bit eccentric. He greeted me outside. "Nikki! How are you, come right in!" Nikki was the alias that I used. It was a short variation of my middle name, Nicole.

Rich gave me a tour of his home. He had a large backyard with fruit trees. The inside of the home was sparsely decorated and hardly had any furniture. He had back drops everywhere; this made for a good shoot location.

After the tour of the house, he said, "Hey, I have something to show you!" We went to his office and he took out his laptop. He then showed me a few pictures that he took of models he had worked with in the past and present. He showed me photos of another young black model that he said he got published. She had curly hair, huge boobs, round hips, green eyes, and a beige complexion. She was pretty, but many of her pictures were very suggestive. In one image, she was wearing a white string bikini; in another pose, she was topless holding her hands over her breasts. He said that he had managed her and gotten her featured in magazines.

"I'm not sure if I want to take pictures like that." I said.

"Before we can shoot, I need to see your driver's license." He then handed me a disclosure that I needed to sign. The form had "Model Release" written on the top. I signed the release form, and we started shooting together. During our first shoot, we shot casual and bikini pictures. Before my shoot, I had brought many cute swimsuits from Macy's. I planned on taking them back to the store after the shoot.

"Why don't you pull the left strap down?" he directed. So, I did. He let me take a look at the photos on his laptop after each outfit. We chose what pictures we liked best after.

"You're a natural model. You have nice skin and don't need a lot of makeup," he said. "Next time bring clothes that are a little sexier."

I set up a profile on a popular modeling website that Rich suggested. I gradually uploaded more modeling pictures. I also started to network with more local photographers and some out of the area. Only a few days had gone by after posting the pictures, and I booked another shoot. This time in Los Angeles. The photographer needed me for a promotional flier. He needed me to take bikini pictures. I couldn't afford to pay for a flight, so he agreed to purchase the ticket for me. On Fridays, I didn't have classes, so I decided to leave to LA then. I called in sick to work and flew to Los Angeles in the morning.

From the airport, I caught a cab to the shoot location. It was an apartment in downtown Los Angeles. The photographer came out to greet me. He was young, in his mid-to-late twenties. He had dirty blonde hair with a 5 o'clock shadow. He seemed pretty nice. We went up to his apartment. It was small. We made some small talk before we began shooting. "So, what makes you want to be a model?" the photographer asked.

"I've always wanted to become a fashion model and wear cool clothes and pose for magazines."

"You're a little too short and curvy to be a fashion model," he said. I came out in my new bikini that I had purchased from the mall. "Cute, but can you take off the top?" The photographer asked. "You can hold your boobs. Perfect! Can you turn around and show me that cute lil' butt. Perfect!"

The pictures came out pretty good. When we were finished shooting, he downloaded the pictures onto the CD for me and called me a cab. I took the cab back to the airport and flew back that same day. I was starting to feel like a real model.

I continued to shoot with Rich. We shot more revealing photos, but I only posted the bikini ones. I even shot some nude images with Rich. He said that he would submit them to editors of magazines in hopes to landing me a paying gig. I had more pictures to post on my profile. I liked the attention that I started to receive. More guys started to direct message me, but I mostly just paid attention to the modeling requests.

One day, someone sent me a direct message that read, "Do you want to make some money posting your photos online?" I went to his profile to check this person out. There were pictures of girls with big booties facing the camera and a catalogue of other girls in suggestive poses. I replied to the message, "Sure, what did you have in mind?"

The person replied and said that they owned a popular urban modeling website based in Houston and gave me the contact number and direct email. From my work phone, I gave the number a call.

I dialed the number, the phone rang, and a guy answered. He had a southern accent and sounded African American. We talked through my lunch hour at work. If I brought my lunch from home, from time to time, I ate at my desk and talked on the phone. He agreed to complete a website with modeling gallery for me if I flew out there for a photo shoot. It sounded like a great opportunity, and he agreed to split the cost of the airfare and arrange accommodations. I arranged to fly out after work on a Friday.

I arrived in Houston, Texas. The weather reminded me of being in Alabama. It was muggy, but warm out and the sky was grey. Dwayne was the name of the photographer that I was working with. He was a black guy in his late twenties, nerdy and tech-ish, like many of the black guys from San Jose. When he said that he would provide me with a place to stay, I didn't bother to ask where. I had to stay in his 1-bedroom apartment.

When I arrived, we looked through the pictures on his computer to get some ideas about our shoot together. We went through the galleries of girls he shot with on his website. I noticed that the same model was in many of the photos.

I finally asked, "You shoot with her a lot?"

"Yeah, that's Lyric," he said. He looked at me up and down. "You're pretty, but you may be too thin to be an urban model." He was a gentleman most of the time. He mentioned to me that he had a sexual relationship with Lyric. She was so pretty, why would she sleep with the photographer?

"Well, I don't do things like that," I snapped back at him. "I'm strictly business."

"Hold on girl!" he said.

"Well I'm just putting that out there," I shot back. I thought to myself, *Maybe I am being a bitch*. But, just in case he had the thought in his mind, I felt it was my job to bring him back to reality. I was not at all into him like that or even considered him attractive. That night, he slept on the couch, and I slept in his room.

The next morning, we woke up early. The weather was still gloomy, warm and humid.

He mapped out a few good locations to shoot. We drove to Galveston beach and shot a few sets there.

The more photos I posted, the more requests for more and more photo shoots. The only problem was that I wasn't making any money. Some photographers offered to pay for travel, but none were offering to pay. I had been modeling for several months now and it was becoming like a second job; a second job that I wasn't getting paid to do. I needed something to set me apart.

Rich called me and said, "You know, if you want to make some real money, I can submit your photos to a friend of mine who has a site."

"What kind of site?" I reluctantly asked.

"Nudes. Girl! You have some sexy pictures on the net floating around." he answered. Where I was just a bit naïve, was not reading over the contract. I signed ownership right of my photographs over to him. He started posting photos of me online, and I didn't receive any compensation for the pictures he sold to websites. 'The model releases the photos to the photographer to do as they please. Sometimes the photographer may submit the photos to magazines,' the contract stated.

Even though I modeled, I struggled with self-image. I enjoyed modeling, but sometimes doubted myself. I applied for a loan and decided to get breast augmentation surgery. The first person I told was my mother. "Well, you're twenty-one years old; you're a grown woman," she said. Mom went with me to my consultation, and she was there on surgery day. I called in sick that following Monday. Luckily, I didn't have class. For a few days after the surgery, I couldn't move.

Later that week, when I felt better, I went to Rich's house and took some updated pictures. Rich submitted them to an editor. Shortly after, I got booked for my first paid shoot. I was offered five hundred dollars from a magazine for a half day shoot. I was so excited. The shoot was for a magazine called, "Blacktail." I went to the liquor store and asked the cashier if they had Blacktail magazine. He pointed to the area on the magazine shelf that was covered by a long piece of cardboard. I open the magazine and started flipping through the pages. The girls were spreading their legs without underwear. There was even girl-on-girl action. I couldn't go through with the shoot. I couldn't imagine someone I knew opening a magazine and seeing me spread eagle.

It was the day of my shoot, and I already knew my decision. The photographer called to confirm the call time. I knew my limitations. The magazine shoot wasn't a good decision for me. It was hard to decline because I needed the money.

"I won't be available for the shoot today."

"Why not?"

"Just had second thoughts."

"Thanks for wasting my fucking time!" Then there was a click and the phone went dead. I knew he had hung up before I could apologize.

The next day I went over to Rich's house to look at some photos that he edited for me. His eyes were red. He shared with me that his house was in foreclosure and that he had to do a short sale. He took a swig of whiskey and asked me if I wanted some.

"No thanks," I said. I told him that I cancelled the shoot.

Drunken and angry he said, "Do you ever want to make any fucking money doing this? What you are not willing to do, the next model will. You keep wasting my fucking time!" he cursed at me. I didn't like the way he way yelling at me, so I left his house. This left me unsure about modeling.

He called later that evening and the next day. I also got a few emails and direct messages from him. I let my phone go to voicemail and stopped responding to email and direct messages that had anything to do with modeling. I figured that if I ever wanted to talk to Rich again, I would make up an excuse later.

Things were going well at work; I had been promoted in my department to HR Generalist. The girl who was in my position prior put in her notice because she was going back to school full-time to pursue a dental career. As the new HR Generalist, I had a new set of responsibilities. I was in charge of administering benefits, hiring, and interviewing; I had less time to chat online. Since I moved out, Tonia and I were back on speaking terms. We both came to the conclusion that we just couldn't live together. Tonia was currently in-between jobs. Since I was now in charge of hiring, I asked Tonia if she would be interested in applying for my old position as receptionist and she said 'yes'. Yet, again I didn't factor in how this would affect our friendship.

Manny walked in to my new office.

"Congratulations!" he said. "If I ask you on a date, you'll probably just file sexual harassment on me now, huh?" He said jokingly.

"No, I wouldn't do that to you."

"So then, what about that date you owe me?"

"How's your wife?" I asked him. As soon as I did, Jim walked in.

"Hi, Tanisha! Hi, Manny! I think they are starting the board meeting upstairs."

Reflection

Throughout my life, I struggled with low self-esteem and spent a lot of time second-guessing myself. Maybe, it was because I wasn't yet comfortable in my own skin. I learned that every decision can bring you to a path of learning and self-discovery.

I also realized that there are institutionalized inequalities that push some women and girls into certain career choices. Some women of color feel like there are no other options. Mainly because they are shown no other options. I learned from an early age that the way you look is everything. Then, society puts girls into categories based on how they look. If you look like this, you can go into these jobs, or if you look like that, you cannot. The modeling industry was the first place where I started to feel like that. According to Black Enterprise, African American women make up only 2% of United States' doctors, but make up 40% of prostitutes. Economic precariousness and stereotypes define women of color as sexually promiscuous and immoral by nature. Brown and Black females are especially vulnerable to sexual exploitation and prostitution.

Many times photographers prey on young women by selling them a dream of fame and fortune. They feed their own pocket books and sexual pleasures by exploiting young girls of color, selling their images and not compensating them appropriately.

If you do not create your own path and do not know where your heading, someone will quickly figure out one for you. You have to create goals and envision a better you.

I started to view modeling more as a hobby than a real paying job. Modeling was put on the back burner for now. My son, my job, and earning my college degree was more important.

Billy and Vernita Walker on their wedding day, in August 1952.

Vernita (Nana) Walker in highschool graduation photo in 1951.

Tanisha's maternal and pertanal grandparents at her parent's wedding reception in 1980. (Left to right) Billy, Vernita, Jonnie & Jerome Sr. Butler.

Lisa Walker in 1980 while pregnant with Tanisha.

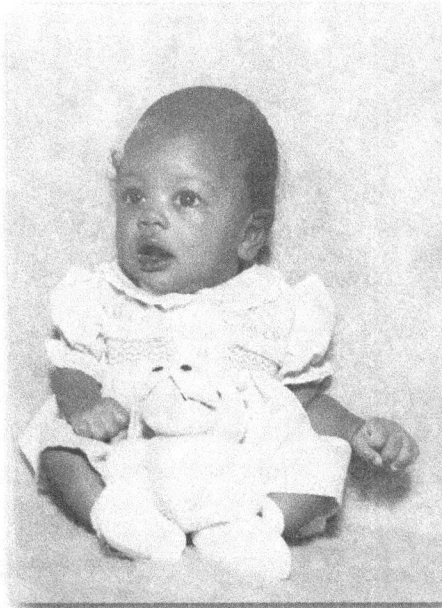

Tanisha Billops as a baby in 1980

**Tanisha Billops and parent's Jerome Jr.
Butler and Lisa Walker in 1981**

Tanisha Billops at age 5, year 1985.

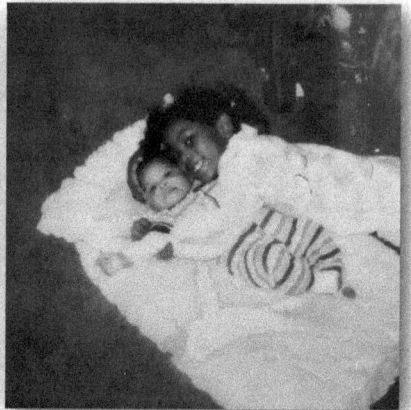

Tanisha Billops and brother
Andre Butler, year 1985

Tanisha Bllops and grandparents Billy and
Vernita Walker at Disneyland, year 1985.

Tanisha Billops, cousins Janessa and Myesha Young and brother Andre Butler in San Diego, year 1989.

Andre Butler, Tanisha Billops and Billy Walker visiting relatives house in Omaha Nebraska, year 1992.

Tanisha Billops highschool photo, year 1995.

Tanisha Billops, year 1995

Tanisha Billops, year 1995

Tanisha Billops highschool graduation photo, year 1998

The "Cali Clique" at Stillman College in Tuscaloosa, AL. Trish, Barrol Tiffany, Porscha, Tanisha, and Kendra (Left to Right), year 1999.

Tanisha Billops and son Cameron, year 2002

Tanisha Billops, year 2002 photo by Bruno Versaci

**Andre Butler, Tanisha Billops and Lisa
Walker (Left to right), year 2005**

**Lisa Walker and Tanisha Billops
on September 28th 2006**

Billy "Grandpa" Walker August 28, 1931 – November 17, 2011

Tanisha Billops at graduation ceremony for teaching credential, May 2015.

Chapter 9

The Sacrifice

I quickly walked into the tall office building. I was meeting Beth for lunch. I only had an hour and fifteen minutes left, so I was in somewhat of a hurry. I walked to the elevator and there was a tall white guy in his late thirties or early forties with blonde-ish orange hair going up at the same time I was. He stopped at the sixth floor, like me.

"Looks like we're going to the same place, ladies first," he said as I walked out. I just smiled and nodded my head, not really paying much mind.

Beth and I went to a little Italian restaurant near her office for lunch. Beth had just started a new job as a receptionist and told me all about it over lunch. I told her that, after going on two years of working at the tech company—even with the new promotion—I was ready for a change. It was hell working with Tonia. Any time I asked her to do something work related she got an attitude. I vented to Beth and she just listened.

After lunch, once I got back to work, Beth called me. I thought that maybe I had forgotten something. "My boss wanted me to ask you if he could have your number," she said.

"Who's your boss?" I asked.

"Remember that guy you ran into while in the elevator?"

"Oh him. He wasn't my type," I said.

"He's nice, has money, and he drives a nice car," said Beth.

"He's old," I said, "and I'm pretty sure he has a wife and kids."

"His name is Jeff, and I'll give him your number," said Beth.

Jeff actually called later that evening. I was correct; he was married with one kid, but the real reason that he was calling was that he was planning on leaving the company that he was working for and was looking for an administrative assistant.

"We're looking for an administrative assistant for our new start-up and Beth referred you," Jeff said. I remembered how I did mention to Beth over lunch that I was looking for a new job and to make more money. I emailed Jeff my resume.

A few days later, one of Jeff's colleagues, Janet, called me for an interview. I was kind of surprised that she called me so soon. I went to the interview the next day at a small office located in Foster City. This was about an hour away from my apartment, but only twenty minutes or so from school. I met with Janet, who's title was Director of Marketing. During the interview, she mentioned that she left her past position as a director with Microsoft to start this business. I told her about my experience and she offered more money than I was currently getting paid, along with opportunities for growth once they went public. The only catch was that they would only be able to give me a six month contract. Funding only lasted through a six month period, but she assured me that by that time, they would definitely have another round of funding.

Jeff was the Director of Sales. The CEO was Jim, and his office was right next to Janet's. Jim was a serial entrepreneur who had started over twenty-five enterprises. Jim co-founded a chain of entertainment facilities featuring games and elaborate indoor mazes that ended in bankruptcy. Now, him, Jeff, and Janet started Fun XS. They would feature conventions held around the world for toy manufacturers. Imagine a big theme park for toys to come to life.

I was ready for a change, so without much consideration, I put in my two weeks' notice. Everyone was sad to see me leave. I felt a little sad too. Was I making the right decision? There was only a total of six people working at my new office, but there were many plans for the company. My job duties were different from my other job. I contacted potential partners, located contacts, and prepared presentations and other marketing material. After a few days of working there, Janet and Jeff flew out to meet with one of the largest toy makers in the United States. I was so excited. I was promised a huge bonus and raise as soon as we signed our first deal, and once the company went public, we would all be rich.

When Jeff and Janet came back from the meeting, after waiting a few days, Janet received an email from the large toy maker that her and Jeff met with. The company said in the email that they liked our company's ideas, but at this time they couldn't make any decisions. They said they may be interested in partnering up in two to four quarters. Two to four quarters meant six to fifteen months away. We didn't have that much time to wait; we only had funding for six months. Janet shared with me that the investors were looking for three to four solid contacts with the largest toy makers in order for another round of funding to be approved.

Jeff and I got to know each other and actually became good friends. When he was in the office, which was one to two times a week, we went for lunch. Jeff's wife was Japanese and he always knew where all the great sushi bars were located. He even called me one evening after work with front row tickets to a Laker game with Shaq and Koby. Every now and then, Jeff would try to flirt with me, but it was as totally platonic friendship. Jeff owned a black Mercedes coup that he let me drive on the weekends from time to time.

"You look better in this car than I do, you should buy it," he would say.

The commute to my new job was starting to put a strain of me. It was a lot further now. The traffic to and from work and to and from school was killer. I was making more money, but with the extra gas and daycare fees, it cancelled out the additional income.

It had been going on five months since I started working at the new place. The team had a meeting that morning. We had a few more meetings lined up with toy manufactures, but so far, all of them said they needed to take a 'wait and see' approach. We were running out of money and needed that second round of funding. That day, Jeff and I went to lunch at a sushi bar not too far from the office. "Some of the investors already want to pull out of the deal. Janet is trying to delay them. The stock market was down and the investors were asking Janet for their money back." I hoped that it was just Jeff being dramatic, but I knew that wasn't the case. Things weren't looking up for the company.

The last couple weeks had been very slow at work. We were approaching that six-month mark, and we hadn't been able to close any deals with a large toy maker. Most of the companies, like Mattel, were still playing 'wait and see' to see if another large company signed with us before they did. In the meantime, Fun XS was running out of money.

My last day at Fun XS finally came. Janet brought me in for a private meeting in her office. She looked a little stressed. She said that they couldn't afford to pay me anymore and that I could file unemployment if necessary. She said that there was still hope for the second round of funding and that if they got it, she could rehire me. She asked me if I could continue to come to the office. I tried coming in for a week or so after that meeting, but decided that with daycare costs and the long commute, it wasn't worth the uncertainty.

I was now unemployed. I needed a job quick. I called into a friend who worked for an employment agency. Hopefully, she had something available. She said that since the stock market was down, hiring was slow. If something came up she would give me a call back. In the meantime, I caught up on a few things. I hadn't seen my friend Michelle, from middle school, since my baby shower, even though we had kept in touch over the years. She came out to San Jose to visit. She pulled up in a brand new white convertible Mustang. Her hair was still long and she looked very fit.

"You look great!" I told her. She came inside my place and we made small talk. "What are you doing these days?" I asked her.

"A couple years ago I started dancing."

"Is it dangerous?" I asked.

"No, we have security at every event. I get booked for parties and things like that," she said. Michelle seemed to be doing great. On the way out, she gave me the phone number to the company that she worked for. When Michelle went home, I considered calling the number. Before I had a chance to call, I got a call from Jeff. He asked if I wanted to meet up and have a cocktail. I hadn't spoken to him since leaving Fun XS.

I pulled up to a somewhat shabby brown building in the middle of a business district to meet with Jeff. The name on the sign said T's Bar and Grill. I walked through the door and saw a stocky gentleman at a podium. He asked to see my ID. The lights were very dim inside the building. I could barely see, but I noticed Jeff was sitting at the bar like he said he would be.

"You didn't tell me this place was a strip club," I whispered to him.

"It's not a strip club, it's a bikini bar," he smiled. Lights flashed and the music blared. Girls walked around scantily clad. To our right, there was a stage with three poles. The DJ got on the mike, "Next up, the exotic beauty, Velvet Rose." There was an Asian girl with hot pink and green dreads on the pole. She performed to heavy metal music. Velvet Rose hung upside down with no hands on the pole. Then, she swung around while taking off her zippered neon half top and exposed her string bikini that barely covered her nipples underneath. I was amazed by the tricks she performed on the pole and thought, *Wow, how did she do that?*

The cocktail waitress came to the bar to take our order. Jeff offered to buy me a drink, but I declined and ordered chicken strips and a coke instead. T's bar was located on one of the main streets in San José. At first glance, someone may have thought it as a restaurant or grill, but as soon as they entered, it was pretty obvious that it was not just any bar. Yes, they served some food and appetizers, but they mainly served booze and women.

Two girls came up to Jeff and I. "Are you here together?" the girls asked.

"We're friends, and I just met him here for a drink," I said. "How are the tips here?" I asked one of the girls.

"The tips are pretty good," she said. "Are you looking for a job?" She asked. The other girl added, "Auditions are on Tuesdays from 1-5pm. You should come."

It was Tuesday, audition day, and I decided to go. I brought Tonia and Porscha along with me for support. Tonia had a few cute pieces of lingerie that she let me borrow. I had a few of my own cute bra and panty sets. I brought my favorite R&B and hip hop songs on a disk to play. I decided to wear black boy shorts with a cute bra and panty set underneath. I stood behind the DJ booth, handed him the CD, and a few customers sat at the bar. Tonia and Porscha sat in the front row with huge smiles on.

I chose a song from my CD and before I knew it, I was working as a dancer. That same evening, the floor manager put me on the schedule four nights a week and told me that I could pick up additional shifts when available.

T's customers included blue-collar workers from the neighboring GM plant, young real estate moguls. Professional and retired athletes made it in from time to time as well. Next to the bar, on the left, was a cabana for "private dances", and on the right side of the club there was a cabana for parties. On the other side of the party cabana was a patio with a few tables.

Starting out, I knew I couldn't do this job forever. It was a "right now" job for money to pay the bills. As long as I took care of my son, provided for him, no one had anything to say as far as I was concerned. I kept Mom updated on my status working at T's, but I told her I was cocktail waitressing. I didn't want her to worry.

I started to enjoy the freedom of not having an 8-5 job. I always hated the taste of alcohol so, I didn't drink and always had awareness of my surroundings. Customers were courteous and treated the girls who worked there with respect. I also made pretty good tips. I only worked four nights a week and fifteen hours less a week than before, but made more money than when I was working full-time. Many of the girls who worked there were college students trying to make it, or single mothers like myself trying to make ends meets, or both. Surprisingly, I even worked at the club with a couple of girls I went to high school with.

One of the girls I met went by the name Toni. She was from the East Bay. She was thin with a caramel complexion. She was cute and appeared to be mixed with something. One night when it was slow, she told me how she traveled quite often between Las Vegas and the bay area.

"I'm going to be taking a trip to Vegas next week, do you want to roll out there with me?" She asked. Even though Toni was cute and all, she was a little rough around the edges. She hung out a lot in Oakland, which was a little different from San Jose. I could tell that she had been taking care of herself for a long time.

"I don't know," I said.

"Girl, it'll be fun! There are hella ballers out there! Way more than this weak ass place!" I hesitated, but eventually said yes. I got a sitter for my son, and we left for Vegas the next night. It was an eight hour drive to get there. We arrived early the next morning. We then spent all day at the Las Vegas DMV getting a permit and ID. This was my first time in Vegas. I didn't have a Nevada ID and that was the only way I was permitted to work at any clubs or casinos in the state.

Toni's uncle was out of town and left us access to his large five-bedroom home. After the DMV, we went straight to her uncle's house and fell asleep. When we woke up, it was around 6:30pm. We got dressed in casual clothes and packed a small carry bag with makeup and costumes and set out for the Vegas Strip. We drove to the club Sapphire, which is a strip club located on the Strip, but their rotation was full for the night. We then drove to Spearmint Rhino, and they had room for more girls in their rotation. This was where we would be working tonight. We went in through the back door, to the dressing room. It was shift change. Girls that worked during the day were leaving, and the evening shift was coming in.

In the dressing room, half naked girls hustled to get dressed. There were so many girls that it was hard to find a place to get dressed. I put on my naughty school girl costume. Toni and I walked out of the dressing room together, but I eventually ended up losing her through the dark LED lights. There was a large bar in the center. This club was way bigger and more upscale than T's. Techno music bumped in the background. Someone gently tugged the white lace garter band wrapped around my thigh for tips. A man and a women wanted me to dance for them. The dancers could go topless here. There were white lounge chairs situated around the club. There were no private rooms and there were several stages positioned around the club. Girls made twenty dollars plus tips per song.

It was now midnight, and we had been at the club since 8:30pm. So far, I had made pretty good tips. After dancing for a while, I was starting to get tired. I looked around for Toni, but didn't see her anywhere. I walked around for a few minutes and couldn't find her. I started getting kind of nervous. I walked toward the back of the club and finally spotted her at a small stage far off to the right, dancing for a black guy in a red shirt. I could see from the distance that she was getting a lot of tips from him. It was dancer etiquette not to mess with anyone's money. So, I stood out of the way until the song was over. Toni saw me, told the guy to hold on for a moment, and got off the small stage before walking over to me. She politely grabbed my hand pulling me towards the stage. Toni introduced me to the guy, "Floyd, this is my girl Coco. Coco, this is Floyd." Floyd was wearing an expensive watch. My grandfather liked watches and growing up he once said, "You can tell by the watch if he has money."

"Want to dance with me?" Toni asked. Toni and I seductively danced another song together on the small stage. Floyd tipped us both hundred dollar bills.

Toni whispered in my ear that we were going to leave with him and meet him at Caesar's Palace Hotel. "Hold on Babe, we'll be right back," Toni said in a sweet voice. Toni pulled me to the side of the stage.

"Why?" I asked, starting to get irritated. I needed to make enough money to cover the cost of the trip plus more to pay my bills. I wasn't in Las Vegas to hang out with some guy. Toni noticed my attitude.

"Girl, it's worth it, I promise," said Toni. "That's Floyd Mayweather!" We made our way back over to the stage where Floyd was waiting. "My girl Coco was looking forward to getting her money for the night."

" I'm rich, don't worry about the money. That's not a problem," said Floyd.

"Okay then!" I said. It was about midnight. Toni and I paid our fees and checked out of the club for the night. We quickly walked off to the rental car.

En route to the hotel, Toni explained to me that she and Floyd had previously met and had messed around a few times before. Once we arrived at the lavish hotel, Toni called Floyd when we were in the lobby. Floyd and four other guys met us in the lobby. We arrived at the huge luxury suite. I asked if I could look around. There were two bed rooms on each side of the suite, each had a hot tub. There was a big living room and eating area with a large table to fit a feast in the middle of the room. There was also a steam room and balcony. It was the biggest and nicest hotel room I had ever been in.

"Order whatever you want," Floyd said. I reached for the menu. Floyd was a very entertaining person. For the next few hours we ordered room service, got in the hot tub, and chilled. Toni and Floyd were chilling in one of the rooms, then came out. Toni was dressed, but Floyd was standing there in all his glory. He and Toni were having a mild disagreement about his lifestyle.

"If you're going to be with other people, you should divorce your wife!" Standing there naked, he asked for my opinion.

"It's kind of hard to concentrate on the question when you're standing there naked," I said.

"I'm not ashamed of my body. I have a big dick and I'm proud of it!" I was shocked by his confidence. He spoke very highly of himself.

Around 9am, he got a call and it was time for him to leave. He and his team packed their things and quickly hustled out of the hotel. I never got the money from Floyd. Toni decided to stay a few more days in Vegas. I took part of my earnings and used it for a plane ticket back home. Vegas was fun, but too much for me at the time. After leaving, I decided that it would be my last time dancing in Vegas. But, I would definitely be back to visit.

It was going on six months working at the club. I felt a desire to get back to a "real" job. I would miss the freedom, limited work hours, and cash after each shift, but I knew that I couldn't make stripping a career for many reasons.

I met up with Porscha and we spent the afternoon in San Francisco. We strolled along the busy sidewalk near Pier 39. We were looking through the shop windows when a young woman with olive colored skin and long brown, wavy hair approached us as we walked past her. "Excuse me, may I read your fortune?" the lady asked while blocking our path down the busy sidewalk. Porscha and I both replied, "No thanks!" and kept it moving. The fortuneteller, this time a little more aggressive, said, "I'll give you a quick fortune for free. If you like, you can get a complete reading for twenty dollars, huh?"

I was still apprehensive. I had never had my fortune told before. I thought about the implications for a split second. There were none, so I said, "Okay." I had a minute to spare. I did have my guard up, ready to walk away if the lady sounded like a quack. We stepped to the side of the walkway where she proceeded with the fortune. The lady examined my palm and, while staring into my eyes with her deep brown eyes and holding my hand, she then told me, "There will be great shifts in your life." She continued, "You will have many great lessons learned during these shifts. You'll soon meet your husband. His name starts with an R." I had to admit that I was a little disappointed with the fortune. I gave her ten dollars for her hustle, and she handed me a blue bar of soap shaped like a star. "Wash with this every night for thirty days and your true love will come into your life."

When I got home that evening, I remembered that I had the soap in my purse. It smelled really good, like lavender, so I thought, *Why not?* I continued to use the blue soap every night until it dissolved into nothing.

A lot of young people who called themselves 'loan agents' came in to the club more frequently with lots of money. I was chatting with a young white guy that came into the club that said he made more than ten thousand dollars per month signing real estate loans. I started searching in the newspaper for possible job openings as a loan agent.

A few days later, a group of young middle eastern men came into the club. Any time anyone walked through the door, like Jack-o-lanterns during Halloween, eyes lurked in the dark in search of a trick. In America, the customers of prostitutes are known as 'Johns' or 'tricks'. The same could be said about men who spent a lot of money in the strip club.

The middle eastern guys requested a private cabana room and a few of us girls to join them in the room. One of the guys in the group of about eight, was tall, looked to be in his mid-twenties with a 5 o'clock shadow, and nicely trimmed haircut. Most of the guys were wearing dress shirts and slacks like they just got off work. I asked the one guy his ethnicity and he said he was Punjabi.

"What do you do for a living?" I asked.

"I'm a mortgage broker," The guy said.

"There are a lot of mortgage brokers that come here. One guy I met said he made ten thousand dollars a month," I said.

"Yes, you can much more than that," he said handing me his card. My name is Manjit, but you can call me Manny," he said.

"I'm actually interested in becoming a loan agent," I told him.

"If you work for me, I guarantee that you make more than ten thousand dollars a month."

I hesitated a few days before calling Manny. I didn't want him to get the wrong impression of me since I did meet him at the club. I really wanted the job though, so I called anyway. The phone rang a few times before he answered.

"Hi Manny, this is Tanisha. I met you a few days ago, and I was wondering if you were still looking to hire loan agents?"

"Umm… Tanisha?" he asked.

"The girl you met at the club. Coco…" I reminded him.

"Oh yes! Hey, how are you doing? I'm glad you called. When would you like to come in?"

"Do you need me to bring my resume?" I asked.

"Yeah sure, How about today at 4pm?"

"Great! See you then!"

I made it to the interview to become a loan agent. The office was located in a large building and was on the third floor. After waiting just a few moments, Manny came out to greet me. He gave me a tour of the office. It was packed with people. It kind of reminded me of the movie Boiler Room, where desks were aligned in rows. The energy in the room was infectious. People looked like they were actually enjoying work. The office suite was about five thousand square feet. Around the "floor", where all the desks were, smaller offices surrounded the main floor. About twenty-five cherry wood office desks were neatly aligned in rows. On top of the desks were black office phones and behind the desks asses sat on leather swivel chairs.

Loan agents called potential clients from stacks of paper title leads. I listened in on one agent's conversation:

"Hello, yes may I speak to Mrs. Johnson. Yes, Mrs. Johnson this is Megan, and I am calling from Community One Financial Services. We work in conjunction with the bank. I'm calling because it shows here that your mortgage is with Wells Fargo Bank and you have an 8% interest rate on your mortgage. My company can definitely lower that."

I enjoyed the energy of the office. There were young, eager people, working and hustling.

I thought to myself, *I could definitely see myself doing this*. I wanted my script to sound even more professional than the girl that I overheard on the phone.

We went back to the office he shared with another guy. Manny introduced me to him as his processor.

"Tanisha, this is Pavon." Pavon was a short, middle eastern guy who wore glasses.

"How does this commission thing work?" I asked Manny. "Is there any way that I can get a salary?" Manny laughed.

"It doesn't work that way," he said. "If you work here, you are an independent contractor."

"What does that mean?"

"That means you are your own boss. You make as much money as you want to and you pay your own taxes," said Manny.

"How do I know if I'll make any money or if this is for real?" Manny then pulled out his check stubs, un-cashed checks, and cash out of his pocket—they totaled thousands of dollars.

"These checks are all from the title company this week! If you work with me, you can make over ten thousand dollars per month easy!" I needed no more convincing.

"When can I start?" I asked.

"How about tomorrow?" Manny replied.

"How about in a few days?" I asked. I needed time to get my childcare plans together.

"That's fine," Manny said. Manny and I shook hands, and I made the decision to start the next week.

I went out to celebrate my new job! Tonia invited me out often, but with my son, school, and working at the club, I was always so exhausted. I couldn't imagine going out. Except for tonight, because I finally had a real job again. I was also almost finished with college. I only had a few more units left.

Tonia and I went to a club on the downtown strip called the Beehive. It was a popular night club in San Jose. When Tonia and I walked up to the door, the bouncer knew her and let us in. We didn't have to pay to get in. I just showed my ID. Once in, we walked to the bar, got a drink, and I followed Tonia to the VIP section in the club. There were many people packed into and around the VIP section. As we approached the section, Tonia introduced me to her friend Keisha and we proceeded to VIP. A guy walked up to us and Tonia introduced me to him over the load hip hop music.

"This is Z. Z, this is Tanisha." The guy was handsome—dark, average height, and very athletic looking. When he walked away, Tonia mentioned that he played for a Bay Area NFL team. Tonia was a bit of a social butterfly; she went out often and knew many people. She even knew a few NFL players whom frequented the clubs. She knew about all the parties and the popular night clubs. She also knew where most of the professional ballers hung out. That's how she met her new beau. Also, Tonia's new friend Keisha invited Tonia to go to exclusive parties with her.

Later that night, when the club was about the close, Z, the guy that I was introduced to earlier, and I exchanged numbers. We started talking on the phone. After doing a little research online, I found out that he was married with children. I called Tonia to let her know.

"Girl, guess what I just found out! Z is married with kids!" I said.

"Unfortunately, most of them are married with families. Girl, let them take care of you! I just came back from shopping at Santana Row. My babe bought me a Gucci Bag and matching Gucci heels!" said Tonia.

I thought about it for a second, but I couldn't imagine being involved with a married man. Mom once told me, "If you mess around with a married man, you're playing with fire." She also said, "When a man starts giving you money, they will feel like they own you." For now, Z was off limits. But regardless, Z was down-to-earth and we had good conversation on the phone. I decided not to mention anything about what I found out. We met up a couple times during happy hour for drinks. I think he was more into me because I wasn't as interested in him—now that I knew he was married.

That weekend Tonia was going to the Oakland Jazz festival and invited me to come. I thought it would be fun and agreed to go. Oakland was thirty minutes down the highway. When we arrived,

Tonia mentioned that she was meeting her NFL beau and that he came with a friend.

"Girl he's your type!" she promised. I was not happy. The last guy she tried to hook me up with was married with three children.

"I didn't come here to hook up with strange guys," I said. I rolled my eyes and felt compelled to ask, "Is he married?"

"No, he's single!"

I had somewhat of an attitude as we parked and walked into the festival. Tonia's beau and his friend stood next to each other. Although I had an attitude, I put on a good front and smiled as we walked up. Both guys were visibly tall, athletic, and stood out in the crowd. They both also had dreads. I didn't like dreads on most guys, but for the friend, it was working for him, plus he wasn't married. Tonia and her beau introduced us. He smiled and said, "What's up?" He said his name was O.J. It was pretty hot outside, but just standing next to O.J., made it feel at least fifty degrees hotter.

We stayed at the festival for about fifteen minutes before going back to Tonia's beau's apartment. He lived near the Oakland pier in a loft apartment. The four of us chilled and talked in the living room for a moment until, Tonia and her man took off. I was now left alone with O.J. We made small talk. He mentioned that her played for a Bay Area NFL team. "So, what do you do?" O.J. asked.

"I'm a cocktail waitress," I answered. At the time, cocktail waitress sounded better than exotic dancer or stripper. "I also just started working as a loan agent." *Damn, I should have started with that*, I thought to myself. "So aren't you going to show me your room?" I asked.

"I'm just staying here for a few days until I move into my place, but let me show you around." O.J. took me to the room he was staying in. I looked around and everything seemed pretty ordinary. I looked at the items on the dresser. His LV luggage was in the corner along with a few other bags. I scanned the room for pictures or remnants of females that he may be involved with, but didn't see any. I sat down on the bed. O.J. sat down next to me and within a few seconds, one thing led to another.

O.J. moved into his own spot in Alameda near the training facility. I came to visit him at his new place. O.J. was somewhat of a homebody in the sense that he focused on his career and didn't go out much—mainly because he was always exhausted after practice. He was different from other guys I had known. For starters, he wasn't married yet, so I knew I had somewhat of a chance. He was successful. He was a few years older than me and had a maturity about him that made me seem like a little girl who looked up to him. I didn't want to seem too eager, so I tried not to call him too often. When I didn't call, I would only hear from him like once a week.

I continued to work at the club in the evenings. I danced at night to earn money until I closed my first deal. I went in one particular evening and the lights in the club were on. One of the girls hustled up to me and said, "The city just came by and ordered Dan to shut the club down." Dan was the owner of the club. "There was a neighborhood petition a few weeks ago, and the city decided to shut us down." The city made the decision because the club was too close to schools and a new city development. I thought maybe God was giving me a sign that I should focus solely on my new job.

With my new company, loan agents sat at their desks and called people from stacks of leads brought by the title company. The leads had the name, address, loan amount, interest rate, and phone number of the person who owned the home. If the person liked what you told them, they were happy to go through the over-the-phone application process to see if we could lower their mortgage payments. Others just hung up, or got an attitude then hung up before even hearing whatever it was you were trying to say. I was actually really good at turning the rude people into clients. I sounded very professional on the phone. I spoke to the people like I was talking to a client who needed this vital information. I had perfected my pitch and pretty much gave the same pitch to everyone—telling them that they had a high interest rate in comparison to their neighbors and the real estate market in general.

One night, I went out; I hadn't planned on seeing O.J. I was at a Halloween party in Oakland.

"Hey what's up," I heard a familiar voice say from behind me. When I turned around it was O.J. I gave him a hug.

"I wasn't expecting to see you out," I said. Later, when I was on the freeway heading home, I got a call from O.J. It had to be about 1am, and I had work later in the morning and had school the next evening. I was only one exit away from my house.

"I want to see you," he said. I did a U-turn on the freeway and went back to Alameda to stay with him. Later that morning, I also had to drop my son off at daycare and go to work. To me, at the time, he represented everything I wanted in a man. In the middle of the season, he transferred from Oakland to Denver.

After O.J. was transferred, I started to miss and wanted to see him. That was the first thing I decided to do with my commission check go visit him; but until I got my commission check, I thought about just putting the plane ticket on my credit card. O.J. almost never called to talk, but I understood he was busy. At times, I almost dreaded calling him because if I didn't ask all the questions and talk there was dead silence. I called him anyway. I brought up the fact that I could come visit him if he wanted. Jokingly he said, "Okay then, come tomorrow."

I answered back, "Okay, then I'll see you tomorrow."

He said, "Yeah right!" He was calling my bluff.

I stopped him and said in a serious tone, "I'll fly out tomorrow to visit."

"I still have to get your plane ticket," he said.

"I'll get my own ticket," I told him.

"What are you rich now?" he asked with sarcasm.

I said, "No, I'm not rich yet, but I will be soon and since when did you start caring about my finances?" I asked him joking. When we got off the phone, I quickly searched for a round trip flight from the Bay Area to Denver for a reasonable price departing the next day. Once I found the flight, I called him back with the flight info. The next afternoon, I arrived in Denver, Colorado.

I was only planning on staying for a day. When I got there, the weather was muggy, but not too cold. I dressed in my cutest pair of jeans and a sexy little white blouse. He was on time picking me up from the airport. He pulled up in a Chrysler 300. I assumed it was a rental. When I got in, he seemed really happy to see me—which was kind of a surprising change because he was mostly reserved and showed very little emotion.

We made it to his apartment. I wanted to take a shower before we went to dinner. While I was getting dressed in the bathroom, I overheard a conversation O.J. was having with someone on the phone.

"What are you going to do for me when I get home?" asked O.J. "What color are you getting the bathroom painted? He asked the person on the other end. *Who is he talking to?*" I was so upset! *No, he is not taking to another bitch!* I said to myself. *I'm going to walk out and sit right next to him.* So I did, and he continued talking. *He is really bold for this one*, I said to myself. His voice tone was sweet and endearing. They spoke about the décor of the one of the bathrooms and paint colors for the kitchen. As I overheard the conversation, I was hurt. I quickly dressed, walked to the couch and sat next to him, so that I could get a closer listen in. As I listened, I heard a guy's voice on the other end. He was speaking to a guy. When he noticed that I was dressed and ready to go, he ended the conversation with the person.

I asked him whom he was speaking to and he told me that it was his roommate in Miami.

The NFL can be like a small community. They were all friends from back in college. His roommate was the brother of Tonia's beau.

After dinner, I forgot about the phone conversation. This was the first time O.J. and I had been on an "official" date. Even though it was just Red Lobster, the fact that he was taking me out was all that mattered.

We woke up the next morning, and it was almost time for me to fly back home. We went out to this Jamaican food restaurant that he spoke highly of, and he dropped me off at the airport. Overall, I had a great time during the trip. Did this mean we were official now?

When I got home, I waited a day or so before calling O.J. "I miss you, do you miss me?"

He replied, "Out of sight out of mind." I was speechless. I couldn't even figure out the words to say. I didn't want to force or convince him to love, or even like me for that matter. *What was I thinking!* We hardly had anything in common, but we did have passionate sex. Someone was bound to catch feelings and it was me. When we talked, he had this matter-of-fact attitude with me; like, why do you try so hard. He was a little older than a professional athlete, and I was this completely smitten girl in love. Regardless of whatever I intended the relationship to be, it wasn't. Yes, he was handsome and successful, but it was clear, he didn't feel the same way about me that I felt about him.

Tonia called me with some gossip she had heard about O.J. He left the team due to rumors about his private life. He was cut and moved back to Atlanta. When Tonia and I talked, it was usually about other people and their problems. This made us forget about our own. Every now and then the gossip was about me.

"Girl, I have some tea for you! It's about O.J. I heard that he left ATL because everyone found out he was fucking around with his teammate." I huffed into the phone and rolled my eyes. I started to think, *why is she always trying to rain on my parade*, but then I thought about it and recalled the conversation I overheard while in Denver. I knew it was time to move on. After that conversation, he made it clear to me that he did not feel the same. He did make it back to the Bay Area a few times, and we did talk on the phone, but I knew he wasn't serious about me. Sometimes, I still thought about calling O.J., because I knew if I didn't, he probably wouldn't bother calling me.

Work life these days was going much better than my love life. I started to get to know the people that I worked with. At my new job, I stayed quiet and to myself. I observed the people and the environment around me. I was on the phone, at my desk making calls when one of the guys whom worked at the office approached me. He was tall, thin, and had a dark complexion.

"Hey, how's everything going?"

"Good," I said.

"So, how do you like working here so far?" he asked. His name was R.L. "Would you like to go out to lunch with us?"

"No thanks, I'll take a rain check," I said. I wanted to fit in some more phone calls during the lunch hour. R.L. was a bit young looking, but cute. When he came into work, he would come by for a quick chat. After about a week or so, I finally took him up on his offer and went out to lunch. We went to a restaurant, that had a tropical theme, near the office. During lunch, we chatted about the loan business, people at the office, and about life in general. He had a nice smile, and his demeanor and openness made me feel like I had known him for a long time. Although R.L. looked young, he seemed much wiser than his years.

When I came back to the office, Heather—a girl who sat near me on the floor—asked, "Are you going out with R.L.? You two make such a cute couple!"

"No, we're just friends," I told her. Heather was one of the people I bonded with at my new job. Heather was a voluptuous white girl with long bleached blonde hair and blue eyes. She was a few years older than me, and like me, she was a single mother. She moved to the Bay Area from Spokane, Washington a few months earlier hoping to start a new life with her son. She sat a few desks behind me. As time went on, we started to talk more often. Heather had a thing for Manny.

Throughout the day, loan agents went outside for breaks. Employees stood on the side of the building near the parking lot to smoke cigarettes and chat. I started to go outside with them, but since I didn't smoke cigarettes, I just would chat it up with people—mainly my boss Tony. Tony was a cool guy. He was a short middle eastern guy with good hair. Before getting into real estate, he was an actor in middle eastern films.

When I started, I knew nothing about real estate. All I knew was that I wanted to buy a house. Manny was my closer, but Tony was the office manager and my boss. Manny was kind of like Tony's protégée. Closers were loan agents, like Manny, who made sure the loan closed after an agent got a client's application. Tony got his start at a company called AmeriQuest Mortgage. AmeriQuest was one of the largest subprime mortgage lenders. Many of the agents he started the office with came from AmeriQuest. Whatever they were doing, they were closing a lot of loans and I wanted to do the same. I was on a mission to becoming a closer.

Between the hours of 12 and 2pm most people left the office for lunch. I found that, actually, this was the best time to call. The office was quiet, there were no distractions, and most people answered their phone during these hours. Tony often would leave with a group of closers. Tony drove a different car almost daily. He had an expensive Porsche, Lexus, BMW, and an SL Mercedes. Many of the closers also drove luxury cars.

Bank officers and title company reps came into the office daily to network, drop off leads, and introduce free promotional office items. Every now and then, Tony would look stressed out. He is the only person I have ever seen puff on two or three cigarettes at a time. He looked like a man who had a lot of responsibility on his shoulders.

From day to day, I looked forward to going into work. R.L. stopped coming into the office. I heard that he had gotten in some trouble. I hoped that everything was okay with him. At the office, people cycled in and out. As long as you were good at telemarketing, you were hired. One of Tony's closers got his broker's license and took a few top loan agents with him. They started a loan company down the way. Tony was pissed. Smoking two cigarettes at a time. I wanted to stay focused though, I knew that this was a different kind of job. The amount of work and energy I put in would determine the outcome that I got in return. I saw firsthand how this worked. The people who stuck with it were the ones bringing in a lot of money.

The mortgage environment wasn't a fit for everyone. There were a lot of young people who worked at the office. We had casual Fridays where Tony would supply alcohol in the evenings to celebrate the week. Many of the loan agents were barely out of high school.

Some of the things loan agents told clients over the phone to get an application weren't always truthful. It kind of made me feel uncomfortable to overhear the deceit being told to clients. Early on, I made up my mind that I would be transparent, honest, and treat my clients with fairness and respect. I couldn't say the same for all of my coworkers.

I quickly found my niche in the loan business. Manny pointed out to me that if I lowered their payments and promised them to "cash out" some of the equity in their home, nine times out of ten the person would refinance. I knew that any rate over 6% on a $500,000 loan was high. Many people that I called had purchased their homes in the 1970's and 80's and had the same loan on their home since it was originally financed. These people had huge interest rates, usually above 10%. I called these kinds of potential clients and took their application over the phone. I made 35% of the origination fee that was charged to the client when their mortgage loan closed. Finally, now in my second month of work, Manny did what he promised and closed two of my applications. I was paid over $12,000 for those two loans. I also had three more loans that were looking good to close in a few days.

After not hearing from R.L. in a few months, he called into the office and someone transferred him to my desk phone.

"What have you been up to?" I asked, happy to hear from him.

"Nothing much, just somewhat in a bind," He said.

"What happened?" I asked him.

"It's a very long story," he said.

Secretly, on my own, I started looking for property to purchase. I knew that I would earn the money to buy a place soon. I just had the feeling. I did it secretly because it was something I wanted to do, and I didn't want anyone trying to talk me out of it. I finally earned enough to put a down payment on the two-bedroom condo that I was eyeballing. I was also graduating from Cal State East Bay, which was a huge accomplishment for me. I was the first member of my extended family—besides distant cousins—to graduate from college. I couldn't believe that after four and a half years, I had finally earned my Bachelor's in Human Development.

Reflection

Some say that professions in the sex industry—such as pimps, brothels, strip clubs, porn, nude modeling, Sugar Babies, website chat porn sites, etc.—diverge from prostitution. Prostitution is known as the oldest profession.

In life, there are many choices. Indecisiveness can lead one to second guess themselves on some of the most important decisions of their lives. At times, I was indecisive, second-guessing myself, especially under pressure. Maybe it was because my self-esteem wasn't genuine. It came from how other people viewed me and not from within. A lack of confidence can hold people back from reaching their full potential.

Chapter 10

Discovering Money

It had been two years since I became a loan agent. After earning my Bachelor's degree, since I was making my career in real estate, I decided to become a licensed real estate agent. After getting licensed, I became more knowledgeable in real estate.

I resigned from my position as loan agent from Community One. After nine months of working there, I found out that Tony was ripping me off with commissions. After becoming licensed, I realized that I was getting less commission than what was stated in my original contract. When I confronted him about it, he dismissed it and said that processing fees and general office fees were being taken out of my check.

Tony didn't take my resignation lightly. Heather and our team of agents were coming with me. When he found out that Heather was leaving too, along with the team of agents we recruited, he kicked both of us out of the office. He also threatened to hold all of my commission checks, even though legally he couldn't do so. So, the next day, I went to Ron—the owner and broker of the mortgage company and explained how Tony was holding my check. Ron understood the gravity of the situation and wrote me a check right there in his office and I left. I didn't want to leave the place where I started my real estate career on bad terms, but I had to do what was best.

I was now working for another company as an official loan closer. Instead of 35%, I now had an 80% commission split. I was making more per deal than ever. My new direct manager was a guy named Al. Al was in his late thirties tall, bald, dark brown complexion. He also used to work at Community One, but decided to leave after he too found out that Tony was ripping him off. When the high pre-forming team bailed on Tony a couple years back, they opened their own office and Al went with them. Al was nice, but he didn't care for Heather too much.

Heather and I were complete opposites, but we made a great team. I was black, and she was white. I was quiet, and she was loud; the list goes on. We eventually started working together to close mortgage loans. Clients liked working with us and referred friends and family to us. Together, Heather and I were closing more loans than most loan agents in the office. Friends and family were seeing how successful I was becoming in real estate, and they too wanted a piece of the real estate pie. Many did try it out, but failed.

It wasn't an easy job, and it wasn't for everyone. Real estate is one of the most important purchases an individual will make in their lives; so at times, customers were difficult.

Anyone who started, in order to have a successful career, had to build their customer base somehow—mainly by telemarketing or networking within their community. A typical loan could take anywhere from four to eight weeks to close; not everyone had the patience to work without pay until a loan closed. My brother, Andre, tried it out for a while and quit after a few weeks. Uncle Keith's wife, Aunt Barbara, gave it a try, but stopped coming in after a few weeks.

To hire, most of the time, Heather and I stuck to placing ads in the paper to recruit independent loan agents. When Auntie Vanessa said that she wanted to give real estate a try, I didn't take her seriously. She recently was laid off from her job at the tech company she had been with for years. She started with me, and Auntie Vanessa was great on the phone. Her first day, she got five applications.

Al approached me in my office. He had an envelope in his hand. "Since you are doing such a great job with your team, here are tickets for an all-inclusive, seven-day trip to Hawaii for two." That was the nicest thing anyone had ever done for me. "I know that you're going to take that white bitch, but it's okay. This is my gift to you."

"Thank you!" I smiled. Off we went to Hawaii! There were beautiful, picturesque views at every turn, but I couldn't help but worry. I stepped off the plane to beautiful Hawaiian women dressed in traditional hula garb handing us leighs. The weather was warm and sunny with a slight breeze. It was definitely a tropical paradise. Mom and Mr. Barnes agreed to rotate the days watching Cameron while I was on vacation. There were moments that I enjoyed myself, but I couldn't stop worrying. I really missed my son.

By the time my twenty-fifth birthday came around, I had made over a half million dollars in real estate commissions. Commission checks came in one after another. Sometimes, I received three or four checks in one day. I went to the bank to deposit a few checks. In amazement the teller asked, "What do you do for a living to make so much money at such a young age?" I normally handed the teller my business card and said, "give me a call if you're interested in an interview."

Heather took a day off of work, so I had some free time. I decided to go to the car lot. The sales man came out, "What can I help you with young lady."

"Hello, I'm just looking," I said, staring at a beautiful silver Mercedes.

"Why don't I get the keys, so you can take it for a spin." The car was forty thousand dollars and I had never even considered purchasing such an expensive vehicle. After some convincing from the salesman I bought the brand new silver Mercedes.

One day, while looking at listings online, I came across a beautiful Mediterranean home. I was ready to upgrade from my two-bedroom condo. My new home had four bedrooms and four bathrooms. The home was in a perfect location—beautifully nestled in the east foothills. It was a fixer upper and definitely needed some work, but it had so much potential. I didn't care too much about how much the remodels would cost; I just knew the home felt right. The home had four large arched pillars that held up a large wrap around deck. There were French doors in the kitchen, master suite, and living room that led to the deck. The view from the house overlooked the San Francisco Bay Area. There were two master suites—one had a large tub with jets and the other, on the lower level, led to a terrace under the deck.

As I started to get more successful, in other people's eyes, my relationships started to change. In terms of fulfilling my goals, I was on top of the world. It had only been two years since I finished college, and I was well on my way to joining the millionaire club.
As far as my love life was concerned, I was dating, but nothing serious.

I was working a lot. I generally got into the office around nine in the mornings and worked until six or seven in the evenings; some days I worked until ten at night, signing loans. I tried to accommodate my clients; some of them worked late or had alternative hours. At times, I worked weekends as well. I was so wired from the full days that, when I finally did get home, all I could think about was what I had to get done or take care the next day. In between all the work, as much as possible, I tried to make time to spend with friends and family. I tried to make time to meet up with my girls for lunch outings. I sometimes even met up with one of my besties to go shopping at the mall or just to hang out. Even though, I felt like there was something missing from my life. I was accomplished, but not fulfilled.

I started going back to church for a while and found solace in the bible. I enjoyed the fellowship and the traditional aspect of the church and Christianity, but struggled with the deeper meaning. Being African American, Christianity was my religion by default. It bothered me the way that they talked about God being this man who is the decision maker of all. I didn't feel like I was separate from God, and I didn't know how to feel about this judgmental guy living in the sky. I knew that there had to be a reason. Everyone's life had meaning. Because I didn't come from a traditional Christian background, it was easier for me to think outside of the box when it came to religion.

R.L. and I still kept in touch. Over the last couple of years we had developed a friendship. He had moved from Memphis in his early teen years and had been raised by a single mother like myself. He had a young son who was exactly a month apart in age with Cameron. Throughout R.L. younger years, his mother moved between California and Memphis. We grew up on the same side of town. He graduated from the high school just miles from mine. We both were into real estate. We always wondered why we had never connected sooner. We talked on the phone often. He would call into my work phone, and I would accept the charges. A couple years back, I found out that R.L. went to jail for the "trouble" that he was in. He was given a three year sentence. For the last part of that sentence, he was able to join a work program with the Department of Forestry where he worked as fire fighter for the department.

It was usually easy to cut guys off, but for some reason, I felt compelled to stay in contact with R.L. He was very knowledgeable and educated. We had a lot in common, but I worried what my friends and family would think of me dating someone with a criminal background. Before he was transferred to the Department of Forestry, I visited him in the county jail. Visiting R.L. was the first time I had ever been inside of a jail. Everything in the jail was grey, except the people. When I visited him, I didn't know about the dress code policy. I had on jewelry, knee high leather boots with heels and a push up bra. They made me take off the jewelry and my boots. The darn metal detector kept beeping. By the time I was finished, I wouldn't have had anything on. Luckily, I had my gym clothes in the car. I went to my car and changed then I was buzzed in through a large electric chain-linked fence to the visiting room. Since he was in the county jail, I had to talk to him through the glass.

Now, I often received cards, letters, and notes in the mail from R.L. In a letter, he asked me to come visit him at camp on his birthday, but I wasn't sure. This time, it wasn't behind glass. Since he was at fire camp, full contact visits were allowed and I could also bring food items. I liked R. L. a lot, but I was apprehensive about visiting. I didn't want to start anything with him or have him get the wrong idea. He had almost two more years left in his sentence. There was just no way that I could have a relationship with him. I finally asked him to stop calling when I started talking to this guy that I met at the gym.

"I have a boyfriend now," I told him out of respect.

"I understand, and I'll respect your "little" relationship," he said.

"But it doesn't mean we can't be friends." After that, he stopped calling and sending letters.

For weeks I heard advertisements on the radio about an upcoming real estate wealth expo at the Moscone Center in San Francisco. The expo was to be headlined by none other than my real estate idol, at the time, Donald Trump, and a handful of other national names like Tony Robbins, Suzie Orman, and Robert Kiyosaki. I was reluctant to purchase tickets to such an event. The tickets were a bit pricy, and I didn't know who would want to go with me to an event like this. I wasn't sure if it would be worth the time and cost.

Later that day, I was sitting in my office when I was delivered a check from a loan I signed. I was surprise because I forgot all about it. *This must be a sign that I need to purchase tickets to the wealth expo*, I thought. It was a rare opportunity. I got on the computer and purchased two tickets to the event. She wasn't sure whom I would bring, but regardless, I was going.

It was 2006 and real estate was a national obsession. Real estate was now floating the economy. Collectively, in the six years since Nasdaq imploded, people relied on real estate as a safe haven for their money. The crowd at the real estate expo was over fifty thousand people. The environment at the expo was high energy. Many of the people I mingled with at the Expo were far from beginners. They were investors who had already invested in real estate, but wanted more information from the experts at the time.

I was sure not to miss Donald Trump speak. I sat in the fourth row and listened to Trump—who my by the way, was paid $1.5 million for his talk. For the first time in my life, I was getting advice from truly wealthy and successful individuals who had accomplished what I was trying to accomplish myself. Trump was the keynote speaker at the event. The speakers did their job and inspired the crowd to go after their dreams. I was totally inspired and was glad that I decided to attend the event. One of my biggest take-aways from the expo was to stop thinking within certain limitations and to think bigger; because success was possible. If the speakers at the expo could do it, anyone could.

The next day, I got up early and started planning my next move as an entrepreneur. I decided that I would start my own mortgage broker-age. Instead of working for someone else, I would continue facilitating loans between borrowers and lenders, but now I would make 100% profit. My business' mission statement was: We work with transparency and aim to educate borrowers to help them understand their loan options. I also decided to specialize in credit repair for borrowers who didn't qualify for a traditional mortgage loan because of negative credit. My goal was to offer my clients exceptional customer service, which would keep them coming back.

I didn't know where to start. I had never started my own business before. I knew that Heather's mother owned a chain of daycare centers in Washington, and Heather grew up helping her mother with the bookkeeping and running the day-to-day operations of the centers. She was truly knowledgeable about running a business. I decided to inform Heather about my plans. Heather was super excited and told me that she would help out any way that she could.

With money, it wasn't difficult to get people to go along with my plans. Since I had the money, but wasn't yet a licensed broker, I found an independent broker who was willing to establish a branch under his license…for the right price. I called the branch office Dream Team Financial Group.

I found an upscale, fully furnished office suite in a prestigious building for rent. In order to have luxury I had to pay the "upscale"price. The monthly rent was pricey, but for the amenities at the time, it was worth it. The office had way more amenities than I had anticipated— a fully furnished office with built in phone lines and a receptionist. The office building was next door to a large convention center where there was always foot traffic. The office suite was located on the seventh floor of the building. The building had a large, beautiful lobby with a waterfall and a coffee shop. This new office space had all the amenities, and more, that I desired.

On average, Dream Team Financial Group closed about twenty real estate deals a month. I made anywhere from $2,500 – 20,000 per deal. And now, with 100% commission I was seeing more money for each deal that I closed. Heather worked as my assistant. She was very organized; she helped by taking care of the office administrative work while I was mostly in the field closing deals.

Heather and I hung out often. I considered her a good friend. She had been seeing Manny for a few years now and things weren't going well between them at all. She confided in me often and valued my opinion. She also had some insecurities about her weight, but she was a beautiful woman. She constantly complained about all the rude things Manny did and said to her. Without being disrespectful, I tried to be as honest as possible; especially when it came to advice about her and Manny. Heather was fun to be around, but at times she could be an outright bitch. When things didn't go right, she would go through depressive cycles, where she was extremely moody. Heather came into the office wearing her over-sized sunglasses.

Oh Lord! Here we go, I thought to myself. "Hey Heather!" I called out, hoping that some of my positive vibes would spill over to Heather.

"Hey…" Heather replied in a short manner. Jeff from Countywide came in and said that we could resubmit the Jones loan. "Okay," she replied.

When I wasn't at the office, I was on the go. When I wasn't on the go, my mind would race, and I would think random thoughts about all the things that I had to do. I also was a little lonely; since I was working so often, I didn't have time to date. Working so much, some important things got pushed to the side and even neglected. I surely didn't have time to cleaning, so I hired a cleaning service to do it for me.

I got tired of hearing, "Girl, you have everything but a man!" Although I had accomplished a lot, I still had a feeling that there was something missing.

I was surprised to receive a letter in the mail from R.L. I hadn't spoken to him for months. In the letter, he said that he was doing well. He also asked if I would come visit him. I really did miss talking to him, the letters and phone calls. I decided I was going to visit RL.

The facility was located near Yosemite National Park. It took over three hours to drive there. I drove alone and didn't mention the trip to anyone. Once I arrived, I started getting a little nervous. My palms had started to sweat. I dressed accordingly and even brought extra cloths just in case they made me change. I got through the metal detectors, this time, no problem. I sat in a room filled with tables aligned in rows. There were also two televisions in the room. A Hispanic family and a middle aged white woman waited for a visit.

R.L. finally came out. He looked better than I had remembered—smooth chocolate skin, clean shaven with a freshly lined fade. He still had his beautiful Colgate smile and little dimples under his eyes. R.L. came and sat next to me. He smelled good, like Dove soap.

"You've been pretty persistent throughout the time I've known you," I said with a huge grin on my face.

"You're very special; since the first day I saw you walk into the office for your interview, wearing that black skirt, I knew I wanted you," he said.

My heart started racing. The vibe between R.L. and I was so strong. Ever since the first day I met him at the office, I instantly latched on to his caring and sensitive manner. He actually listened to me when I talked. He was interested in me and wanted to know more about me. It made me smitten and we had never had sex. He was the first guy who seemed to really be into me and not just for sex. We talked about so many things during the visit. We talked about taking our boys on a playdate once he was home.

I wanted to better understand the bible, so I purchased a student bible and devoted myself to reading it an hour before bed every night. I started to pray more often. I thanked God for my many blessings, but I prayed that God would send me a husband.

R.L. sent me a card that read:

Dear Tanisha,
You're smart, ambitious, and most of all a great friend.
I look forward to taking you out and do-
ing for you the things that you deserve.
Maybe one day I can give you that wed-
ding in front of the Disneyland Castle.

Sincerely,
R.L.

I met up with two of my girlfriends for lunch. I showed them the card. "Girl, when my dad was in jail he use to do the same thing. We got a card every week and when he came back after a few weeks he was the same asshole! That's nothing but jail talk." Said one friend.

I visited him twice after that, and we talked on the phone every day. I had to see if he was the "full package." I told my mom about my new boyfriend. Others knew R.L. as this secret boyfriend that they had only heard about and never met. R.L. brought up marriage.

He asked me if I could pick him up once he was released. I wanted to experience a relationship with R.L. So I said yes. I also decided that it would be nice to meet his mother and go out to lunch. The next week I went out to lunch with R.L.'s mother Pat. I really enjoyed the outing with Ms.Pat and was excited to tell R.L. how about the outing..

Some of my friends knew the real deal about R.L. My family just assumed he lived far away. I knew they wouldn't be supportive of the fact that I was dating him if they knew the truth.

When I picked him up, I felt like my life would be different from this day forward. I knew R.L. was the man I wanted to spend the rest of my life with.

When we woke up the next morning, I knew that R.L. was the man of my dreams.

R.L. was passionate and told me the things that I wanted to hear. We wanted so many of the same things I did.

R.L. and I got married on May 5, 2006. We opted to get secretly married. The only people who were there was Mom, Pat, R.L. and I. It was nothing fancy. We were married and the only thing that mattered to us was that both our mothers supported us and were witnesses to our marriage. May 5, 2006 was one of the happiest days of my life.

I took the day off, but came into the office and told Auntie Vanessa and Heather, "Surprise, We got married!"! I announced as R.L., mom, and MrS. Pat walked into the office. They were both somewhat shocked. We planned on having a bigger ceremony with friends and family the following summer.

R.L. was experienced in real estate—Heather knew him from Community One—so I didn't think twice about having R.L. work at the office while getting on his feet. When I met R.L., he was at the top of his game; there was never any doubt in my mind that he would bounce back.

R.L. was only coming into the office part-time since he was taking some college classes in the morning to get a certification. Most of the time, he stayed low key and did his job.

I didn't consider how Heather might feel about the whole thing—me getting married and R.L. working at the office. As far as I was concerned, it was my business, and I could hire who I pleased. R.L. did come into an all-female environment and there were times when the claws were certainly out.

I started feeling this weird vibe from Heather. She had also started to show passive aggressive behavior. She didn't tell me how she felt. We started to have a huge disconnect. She even gave me the silent treatment for a little while. I could tell she had a problem with me. I felt like I was back in middle school. R.L. just suggested that I ignore it. "She'll come around," he encouraged. For some reason, I wasn't sure if she would get used to the fact that R.L. was here to stay.

One of R.L.'s clients, whom lived in Los Angeles, was interested in refinancing her home through one of Washington Mutual's loan programs. Fixed and Adjustable rate mortgages offered by Bear Sterns and pick-a-payment loans offered by Washington Mutual, as well as second mortgages by Countrywide, were the biggest financial products we sold. Mortgage lenders, like Bear Sterns and Countrywide, came up with new loan programs and some of the homeowners who didn't qualify for a mortgage loan, now did. These lenders gave mortgage brokers points. Points were under the table commissions paid to the broker, in addition to the commission they already made from the borrower.

R.L.'s client's loan was approved. Heather and I decided to make the five-hour drive to sign the loan as opposed to having a traveling notary go sign with her. This was a special client because it was a pretty good size loan amount, and she was the manager of a renowned celebrity hair salon on Rodeo Drive in Hollywood. I was at the height of my career. If I could get some celebrity referrals out of R.L.'s client I would strike gold. We arrived on the infamous Rodeo Drive. We parked on the rooftop of the building the salon was located on and walked down the dap cement stairs. All I could think about was, *this is the best day of my life!*

The loan signing went great. R.L.'s client loved us! We met the owner of the salon. He was tall, African American, and had dreads. The salon owner was so nice! He took us on a tour of the salon, gave us a free copy of a book he published, and invited Heather and I back to the salon whenever we came back to Hollywood. We even met a celebrity client of his who was there getting her hair styled. I knew for sure I would get referrals from this signing.

Reflection

Money has been known as a "good evil" and it plays a different role in each individual's life. At times, money has played various roles in my life. Like from not having enough, to having so much of it that I had no real plan of what to do with it. After a few years of working in a booming real estate market, I had made a small fortune and was now able to afford things differently than I had in the past. I also started to change the way I thought. For once, I felt in control over my own destiny.

I also longed for love. I literally dreamed of having a husband. With the big house, cars, and money I wasn't truly happy alone. I was looking for more of something. I thought that once I got the business I would be happy. Then it was once I got married, that I would really be happy. Unfortunately, none of those were the long term solutions to the emptiness that I felt.

Chapter 11

The Trade Off

I got along well with my mother-in-law, Ms. Pat. Although we went to lunch once, I had mainly gotten to know her through three-way-phone calls between her, R.L and I. Ms. Pat was Southern bell with a good sense of humor. I could tell that Ms. Pat had lived a hard life that taught her many values. Even though, she still had a great spirit and always possessed a positive outlook. Her and R.L. were pretty close. He was the baby of the family. His brother and sister were more than thirteen years his senior. Pat once said, "Ooh Chaald! If R.L. didn't get his way he would have a fit!" She always had a humorous story to tell about her son. R.L.'s family called him Scooter, but Pat called him lil Robert. His father was Haitian, but R.L. didn't like to talk about him much.

Grandpa's RV easily packed ten to twelve people inside. The beach was just a thirty to forty-five minute drive away from picturesque beaches in Monterey, Santa Cruz, or Half Moon Bay. For Mother's Day, 2006 we all went to the beach to celebrate. Everyone came out; Pat, R.L, my mom, cousins, Nana and Grandpa Billy. We all had a great time. R.L. and I were newlyweds. Our family barbecued under the warm sun and reminisced about old times. Grandpa played his jazz music. It was either Miles Davis or John Coltrane.

Visiting the beach was like an escape from reality. It was situated in a narrow valley overlooking Monterey Bay. There were many people playing in the salty water—kids and adults. The beach was a shimmering expanse of endless white that cushioned the ocean's timeless arrival—bringing with it the seas flotsam to decorate the sands soft bed. The glare from the sand reflecting the sun's rays was blinding and causing people to stroll along the genial sloping beach with eyes screwed almost shut.

Pat spent the last week in May with us at our house. Most of the days she stayed with us, we went shopping and out to dinner. I viewed her as not only a mother-in-law, but as a friend. After the week was over, R.L.. dropped his mother off at home in Modesto. That day, Heather and I hit the road to sign the loan in Los Angeles.

After signing the loan, Heather and I were now heading back to San Jose. While on the highway, I returned a few phones calls. I had a missed call from Ms. Pat. I hadn't spoken to her in a couple of days since RL dropped her off back at her house. I tried calling her back, but there was no answer.

After the five-hour drive, I finally made it home. "Babe! I'm home," I called out to R.L. R.L. came out from the other room and gave me a kiss.

"My brother's coming out from Modesto. When he gets here, let's shoot up the freeway to Ben's Burgers for lunch," R.L suggested.

"Sure!" I said. *Nothing sounds better than a nice, juicy cheese burger*, I thought.

After about thirty minutes or so, R.L.'s brother, Quincy, arrived at our home along with his new girlfriend. The burger joint was located in Oakland, so we drove up the interstate 880 freeway. We were driving in the lane closest to the center divider driving North. On the left side of the highway, a late year Toyota sedan was going the opposite direction, going South on the interstate. Just as we passed, the sedan swerved and flipped into the air. The vehicle landed on its back. As smoke filled the interstate, the vehicle slowly spun around as oncoming traffic narrowly escaped hitting the vehicle. RL was driving and slammed on the brakes in my silver Mercedes. RL then proceeded to jump out of the car, over the center divider, and into oncoming traffic. It was all happening so fast that I just sat in the passenger seat. The driver was trapped inside the car. R.L. reached into the car, pulled out the driver, and helped her safely to the side of the interstate. The driver was an older Hispanic lady. Blood streamed down her face. R.L. then ran back to the car and retrieved her purse. At this time, other pedestrians had started to stop and a man who was a doctor came to assist.

R.L. hopped back over the divider and into the driver's seat of our car. The three of us watched while R.L. preformed this heroic act. R.L. was very modest about it, "I learned that at fire camp," R.L said. We all talked about the event the rest of the day and even during lunch. We laughed and joked calling R.L. a Power Ranger and Super Hero. We also talked about how none of us has spoken to Ms.Pat in a couple of days. That wasn't like Ms. Pat. She was always in touch with one of us. "Maybe she went to visit Aunt Joy?" R.L suggested. "Is that like your mom to leave out of town and not let anyone know?" I asked R.L.

It had been a long day. We got home later that evening, still a bit shaken up from the accident on the highway. I went to the restroom and left my phone in the living room. From the restroom, I heard my phone rang, then stop. Then, it started ringing again. It kept ringing none stop. My phone rang often, so it wasn't anything abnormal. It may have been a client with a questions, Heather, Mom, one of my loan agents, or a friend wanting to chat it up. When my phone finally stopped ringing, I heard my husband's phone ring. "Babe, I think you should get that." I called out to R.L, but he was in the other restroom down the hall. "Can you grab it for me?" he asked. I hurried out of the restroom and grabbed my phone then his.

Looking at his cell phone screen, "It's your brother!" I yelled out to R.L. I felt a pang in the pit of my stomach. Before Quincy left, he said that he would go check-up on Ms. Pat. Something wasn't right. "Hello," I answered.

"Tell R.L. his mom is dead!" said Quincy's girlfriend on the other end of the phone.

"Wait hold up. What?" I asked confused. My brain couldn't register what I was being told. "Is she hurt or in the hospital?" I asked.

"No, she is dead!" R.L. was now out of the restroom.

"What happened?" he asked. I hesitated to say anything. All I could do was hand R.L. the phone.

"No!" R.L. yelled into the phone when he heard the news.

What normally took us over an hour to drive, took us only thirty minutes. The whole way to Ms. Pat's house was like a daze. R.L. sped down the freeway at 130mph. When we got to there, there were no rescue vehicles present. Inside, two of Ms. Pat's neighbors were inside the house trying to lend their support. Quincy and his girlfriend were sitting on the couch sobbing, looking like two deer in the headlights. "Where is Momma?" R.L. asked out of breath, like he just run up thirty flights of stairs.

"The coroner is on the way," the neighbor whispered to me.

"I'm so sorry sweetie," said the another neighbor. R.L. ran to his mother's room, and I was right behind him. When we got to the bedroom, I couldn't believe my eyes. There Ms. Pat was lying on the right side of her bed with a bible opened faced down at her side— opened to Matthew 6:9. I looked at her face; she was clearly deceased. This was the first time I had ever seen a dead body besides at a funeral. The ceiling fan above the bed was on and made a slight scraping sound with each turn. Her table fan was still on as well, sitting on a stand near the window. R.L. was completely distraught.

"Turn that shit off!" R.L yelled. I unplugged the fan, but the ceiling fan kept spinning. With anger mixed with sadness, R.L. pulled the ceiling fan out of the ceiling. With a crash, the room went dim. "My mom is gone T!" RL cried out.

The first neighbor came into the room. "Honey, calm him down," she insisted. I wasn't sure what to do; I had never seen him this upset before, and rightfully so. This was my first real experience with death. In the past, I had been to funerals for old, distant relatives that I never really knew. But, this was my first time experiencing the death of someone I loved and spoke to daily. I was shaken to my core.

I helped arrange Ms. Pat's funeral services. The family asked if the service could be held in her hometown of Memphis, Tennessee. R.L.

and I flew to Memphis for Pat's final resting place. Robert was in full grief mode. It was hard for him to understand how his mom could be gone so soon. I felt sadness and heartache for R.L. because I knew that Ms. Pat was one of the most important people in his life. Anxiety about the future started to set in.

A few uneventful months had passed since the funeral. Heather and I still experienced our ups and downs, but nothing out of the ordinary. Every so often, when ever Heather came into the office with her huge Christian Dior, Audrey Hepburn inspired sunglasses, it meant she had been crying, or didn't get enough sleep. When she wore her sunglasses, I instantly knew that it had been a long night, and it was going to be a bad day.

Heather wore a straight, "Don't fuck with me face," that went along with the glasses. I knew not to say a word except for, "Hey!" I was lucky if I got a nod or reply back. Her mood swings started to drain me, and I started to get annoyed and tired of walking on egg shells when she was in one of her moods. It had been almost three years since Heather began seeing Manny. Frankly, I was tired of hearing all the stories about how mean and disrespectful he was to her. I was getting fed up! Any problem between her and Manny was becoming everyone else's problem.

I had a few loans that needed to be submitted, plus I had been having some trouble sleeping, so I decided to get into the office early one morning before everyone else. I walked into the dime office and noticed there was something different. I switched on the lights and to my surprise, Heather's side of the office as completely empty. Her photos, office supplies, and personal office mementos were all gone. Instantly, my blood began to boil and the water started to swell in my eyes. That BITCH! I thought. Even though I knew she would never steal from me, I checked my side of the office to make sure none of my things were missing. While doing so, I found a letter in my desk from her. Any explanation for bailing on me and my business wasn't good enough. Without reading the letter, I balled it up and threw it in to the trashcan.

With heather gone, I was working more, but realized that I didn't have to deal with her moody ass anymore. I was so angry with her, and I felt like she had abandoned me. The non-stubborn part of me, deep down inside, missed her humor and the energy she brought into the office when she was in a good mood.

I didn't dwell on Heather leaving; I continued to do what I needed to do to manage the day-to-day operations of my business. I had to do my job along with Heather's. I was falling behind on submitting some loans. I had plenty of business, but cash in the business account was running low because deals weren't closing fast enough. I finally found someone to hire in Heather's position. That was another expense that I didn't anticipate.

I decided to ask Nana and Grandpa Billy for a personal business loan of a substantial amount to cover a couple of months' worth of business expenses while I focused on closing the loans in my pipeline. I knew they had the money since they had just refinanced and took out a six figure amount.

It was now 2007, and home prices were dropping pretty much everywhere in the Bay Area and surrounding locations. While I submitted loans, I noticed that more often than not, past clients were getting turned down because they no longer had enough equity in their homes to refinance at a lower interest rate. Many of my clients depended on the money from their mortgage loans and lines of credit to live so they would refinance every 1-2 years. I had many clients who, like clockwork, would call every year or two wanting to pull cash out of the equity in their homes out of necessity. Also, interest rates were starting to rise. The main problem was that lenders were denying customers because their homes were losing value and not appreciating. I even started to hear about past clients defaulting on their home loans. A couple years' prior, Al had warned me that we were in a huge real estate bubble that was about to burst.

One day, a bank rep from Washing Mutual came into the office. I had done a lot of business with her in the past, so she was a pretty creditable person. She told me that some loan agents from my old office were subpoenaed to court for shady loans. The bank rep said that angry clients were demanding their original loans back and calling into the office wanting to speak with the broker.

R.L. hadn't been dealing with the passing of his mother well. He was depressed most of the time and hadn't been out of the house much. I decided that we should go out. While out, we stopped by Nana and Grandpa's house, as I did regularly when I was on that side of town. I pulled into the driveway of the south side home and instantly noticed that the grass in the front yard was flooded. R.L and I got out of the car to see where the water was coming from. That's when we spotted Grandpa Billy in his RV yelling at someone.

Nana was pleading with Grandpa Billy, "Come out of the RV Billy. Please come inside. Look Billy! Teesh and R.L. are here." She said hoping that would make Grandpa Billy snap out of his possessed state. Grandpa continued to curse "You black Nigga! You look like a monkey," he cursed in the dark RV.

'R.L. can you help me get Billy in the house?" Nana asked. Grandpa Billy finally went into the house. He looked dazed and confused. Once Grandpa Billy was safely in the house and everything settled down, we left wondering what was going on with him. Shortly after that incident, Nana announced to the family that Grandpa Billy was diagnosed with Alzheimer's.

These days I was working more hours than I ever had. Expenses seemed to be getting more expensive. Despite the warning signs that real estate may be bottoming out, I still tried to remain optimistic about the real estate market. I was noticing that I didn't have the same energy I once had. I was becoming tried more often. I just felt worn out. I started to feel sick to my stomach. At first, I was in denial, but soon I recognized the symptoms. I took a pregnancy test and it came up positive.

Jorge from Countrywide came into the office one day.

"Did you hear about Bear Sterns?" he asked concerned.

"No, what about them?" I asked.

"They are no longer accepting subprime loans," He told me.

"What? That can be true. I have like twelve loans with Bear and all but two are prime," I replied in disbelief.

"Well, I'll see what I can do with them?" said Jorge, trying to drum up some business.

"Hold on, let me call our rep." I said to Jorge.

"Anything you have with them, give it to me so I can see what I can do?" After I made my call, I found out that what Jorge said was true. Bear Sterns couldn't process ten of the loans that I had submitted to them.

At a time when I was supposed to be happy and blissful, I was stressed and distraught. Being pregnant at a time when my business was going down the drain brought me more feelings of anxiety, stress, and uncertainty than I could even explain in words.

Until now, I was able to bury some of my emotions in work. I buried my anger in determination, while my anxiety was over shadowed by tenacity. Now that everything was unraveling, I was faced with these buried emotions coming to surface. At first, I tried to think of life as lucky verses unlucky—that you are either rich or poor. Maybe I was going through an unlucky streak. Or even worse, maybe I was meant to be poor. I started to have conflicting emotions daily. I worried about how was I going to pay my grandparents back. Bills at the office started to outgrow the income that I was bringing in. I was now at the brink of financial ruin, when just a few months prior, I was felt on top of the world. I felt like I was watching an approaching train wreck and it was too late to do anything about it.

I went over the Nana and Grandpa's house to let them know that it would be a few months before I could pay them back. During that conversation, Grandpa accused me of overspending and purchasing lavish items with the money that he loaned me—even though this was not the case. Members of my extended family started to get involved. Since Aunt Vanessa worked with me, she tried to mediate the situation. Others gossiped about the cars that R.L. and I owned. "She should sell the cars or the house to recoup the money that she owes," they said, not understanding the circumstances I was dealing with. They were only making assumptions. The gossip just made matters worse.

The money I owed my grandparents strained the once close relationship we had. They couldn't understand why I didn't have the money to pay them back right away. I had rent at the office and other bills that came with running a business. I had so many things on credit with such a high overhead, that I was in the red. Bills outweighed the income that I produced. R.L. and I also had expenses at home that we had to keep up with.

As Grandpa's Alzheimer's progressed, he got more agitated with the fact that I owed him money. Even with a memory disintegrating from disease, one thing Grandpa Billy didn't forget was when he was owed money. Nana became more stressed as Grandpa became more agitated. One day, Grandpa called me and said, "Where's my money you little bitch!" Shocked, I hung up the phone without saying a word. I was confused and devastated.

As I sat down to use the toilet, deep burgundy blood dripped into the toilet, and I felt a mild ache on my left side. *I'm having a miscarriage*, I thought to myself. I tried to mentally prepare myself for the possibility of one. I knew a person could only go through so much stress while pregnant. It was bound to happen. I drove to the emergency room.

"The baby's heart beat is strong. The ER doctor pointed out on the monitor. I smiled and knew at this point my baby was going to be okay. The doctor continued, "I think it would be wise to continue to monitor you and your baby weekly." I was put on best rest for the next couple of days.

At home, I started receiving delinquent notices for late bills. I had to pay the bills at the office to keep money coming into the household. I was so stressed that I couldn't bear to even open the notices. I gathered them, put them in an empty Louboutin shoebox, and stuffed them under the bed. As I was doing so, I realized that one of the letters was a payment demand from my grandparent's attorney. Now, my own grandparents wanted to sue me! I started to cry. I was devastated and felt like a failure.

Within a couple of months, things went from bad to worse in the real estate world. Mortgage lenders and banks crumbled. Lending dried up and so went my income. It was kind of like a domino effect. I could no longer afford the rent at the office. I gave my loan agents the heads up. The landlord gave me one week to come up with the rent or vacate. I had to vacate the office.

Less than a year later, most of the lenders who I submitted loans to on a daily basis were out of business. This list included many other real estate offices, title companies, lenders and other businesses that catered to the real estate industry. After I closed the doors to my business, I felt a sense of relief. I was no longer under the pressure of having others, outside of my family, rely on me. At this point, I couldn't rely on myself to make things happen.

I found a job as a real estate agent for a high-end luxury real estate firm. I figured that rich people still had money. I had to deal with arrogant attitudes from some of the real estate agents who worked there. I specialized in real estate loans and refinancing, and there weren't many people who were in the market to purchase multimillion dollar homes. I had to build my clientele from scratch.

I started hosting Open Houses for other agents in the office. This was a way for new real estate agents to market themselves. New agents were required to drive to a home listed by a lead real estate agent, put the Open House signs out around the neighborhood, and then spend the next 5 hours of their Saturday or Sunday greeting and handing out business cards or fliers to prospective buyers. The new agents were given lower end homes, not the multimillion dollar homes. These homes weren't staged and most of the time had no running air-conditioning. It was summer time, and I was pregnant. My desire to continue working there didn't last long.

At one point, I joined a multi-level marketing firm that manufactured and distributed products made from blended fruit juice concentrates, powders, and purees. Come to find out, the company was the subject of several controversies. I didn't last long here either.

I then attempted get another business started. This time, at a loan document processing company. Many real estate agents were inundated with short sale listings. Home prices were dropping so rapidly that owners were now selling their home for a loss. For a fee, my new company would help real estate agents process short sale documents, while helping homeowners who were underwater in their homes and requesting loan modifications for cheaper payments.

I made a website, fliers, and business cards, and visited real estate offices and title companies in the Bay Area pitching my business. Many real estate agents had files of customers who needed help modifying their mortgage loans and were interested in working with my company. After doing about a week of marketing, I had twenty files. I started getting to work right away. I called banks and mortgage companies and sat on hold for hours. When I wasn't on hold, I was transferred from one customer service agent to another. I faxed in documents and paperwork to them. Customers could have done this task for themselves, but most just didn't have the time or patience.

Luckily, one of the job agencies I contacted early on, after closing the doors to my business, called me about a position in the mortgage division at a retail bank. It was a temporary position, the manager was leaving on maternity leave, but with my professional background they knew I was an excellent candidate for the position. I hid my baby bump under a cute button up, and a navy blue blouse with black pencil skirt. I went in for the interview and they loved me. I started work just a few days later.

I eventually let the staff know I was pregnant. When the manager came back from her leave, I was ready to go on mine. I did all of this while I was still under observation from the doctor. I had developed preterm labor. Before starting the job at the mortgage company, I was hospitalized for three days. This is when I was told I had gestational diabetes and high blood pressure. He put me on bed rest and told me to take it easy for the rest of the pregnancy. I couldn't rest. Since I had been self-employed, I had no medical benefits, and both R.L. and I had to be bringing in income just to pay the mortgage. As stubborn as I was, I worked up to a week before I gave birth. Luckily, the baby was born just two weeks before her actual due date and no sooner. R.L and I welcomed a healthy baby girl on a rainy November night. We felt so blessed to be parents.

After the baby came, it was weeks before I could go back to work. R.L. maintained the finances as much as he could. He found a new job driving trucks and delivering large appliances to new home developments. Unfortunately, his salary wasn't enough to cover the debt I had amassed over the years. I was in so much debt from going out of business, that I had no other option, but to file bankruptcy in order to save our home.

R.L. was working and away from the house more often. I was at home with the baby. I began to become resentful that R.L. could just come and go as he pleased while I, on the other hand, had a baby attached to my hip. I was still passionately in love with R.L., but he and I started to argued almost daily. In reality, I was bitter about losing my business and being in debt. He was stressed because we had a new baby, and as I was unraveling, he had to hold it all together.

When I started to get my energy back, I decided that I wanted to start another business. This time, a nanny agency for busy parents. I would provide verified home childcare and midwives for busy parents. I started the business with a lot of momentum. This was going to be my come back! I worked from my home and advertised online and in a parent's magazine. I got up and running, but expected an immediate return on the money I had invested. Where did I go wrong? I decided to do other things out of the office. I didn't know much about the home help industry, but as a working parent knew that having such a service would be very helpful. It didn't take me long to find customers, but finding reliable staff was a different story. After awhile, the momentum that I had when I started faded. I hadn't found any reliable staff. I started getting discouraged after a couple of weeks of interviewing person after person, and decided to move on to something else.

Grandpa Billy's memory was fading fast. Sometimes he forgot my name and most of the time he forgot that I owed him money. It was 2008, and Barack Obama had won the presidential election. He had become the first black president of the United States. I followed the election closely, making sure that I cast my vote in the primary election as well as the main election. I sat next to Grandpa Billy watching CNN. He sat quietly glaring at the television. "Aren't you happy that Obama won Grandpa?" I asked him. Grandpa Billy nodded his head and mumbled something. Even though Grandpa Billy was losing his mind, I knew he was aware of the importance of the election. He was aware of most important things; it was just hard for him to verbalize it.

Seeing a family in the White House that resembled mine, gave me a feeling of hope. Hope that others would finally see black people for the content of their character and not like a stain on their shirt. Realistically, I knew that inequalities for minorities wouldn't change overnight, but the fact that they were changing is what mattered the most.

It was just days after New Year's 2009. I hoped to bring in the new year with great new beginnings. R.L. and I celebrated the New Year together. We stayed the night at a luxury hotel in downtown San Jose with a view that overlooked the Silicon Valley. At the last minute, I was able to book a luxury suite for an awesome price. New Year's Eve, R.L and I met up with some friends. R.L. paid for all of us to get into a popular night club within walking distance from the hotel. We partied the night away in the VIP section. That night, I had faith that 2009 was going to be a much better year than the last two years.

Although things weren't perfect between R.L and I, we were managing. I appreciated the dedication that he had to me and the kids. But, at the end of the day, we were both going through our own emotional things. One day, I was happy and wanted to make my marriage work. A day later, I wanted to pack my bags, leave everything behind, and move out of state. I felt depressed, hopeless, and confused. I held onto guilt for losing the loan business. I had a new business that was going down the drain. I blamed my husband for not being able to help me make this debt disappear. I blamed myself for not making better financial decisions. Now, I was a mother with two small children, I felt alone.

I started my job search once again and found one working as an account executive for an internet marketing company. I was making decent money.

A few days after the New Year, I was back to reality. I started to suffer from a kidney infection and was in a great deal of pain. The doctor in the emergency room prescribed me pain killers and antibiotics. I didn't have much of an appetite if any. I also wasn't drinking much liquids. R.L. had to make a delivery for work. Mom came by to see me and took the baby so I could get some rest.

Mom had dropped the baby back off to me later that evening. R.L was now back from work. R.L called his sister to see if she could keep the baby overnight so that we both could get some rest. She agreed to watch the baby. R.L left to drop the baby off. His phone started to vibrate. I realized then that he had forgotten his phone on the bed. I picked up the phone and the text read, "So we going out or what?" I then checked the rest of the messages in the thread. "What's your major?" texted R.L.

"Human Development," was the reply.

"What's that?" texted R.L. "Maybe, I'll come pick you up and take you on a little date somewhere," texted R.L. That was all I needed to see. Images of him possibly cheating on me with another girl flooded my mind. The rage in me was indescribable.

"What the fuck is this?" R.L. said as he saw his clothes pulled out of the closet and dumped onto the floor.

"What the fuck is this?" I yelled, throwing his phone hoping to hit him in head, but he ducked and picked the phone off the floor.

"It's nothing!" he said.

"Who is this girl, RL? You've been cheating on me, I know it!"

"I'm not cheating!" R.L. yelled back. He was trying to explain himself and all I heard was mumbo-jumbo. I couldn't hear anything he was saying. I stomped to our walk-in closet and started to pull his clothes off of the hangers. I opened the front door and preceded to throw them onto the porch. I was so enraged!

"Just get out!" I screamed. "It's over!"

"Stop tripping," he yelled back. "You're making a scene!" R.L slammed the front door closed. I ran back to the room to get more of his things. I wanted him out. Next thing I remember was R.L on top of me. Maybe he was trying to calm me down, but this enraged me even more. What happened next is a blur. I got up and ran out into the garage and dialed 911. R.L. then jumped on his motorcycle and sped away. Before you know it, the police were at the end of our street apprehending him. From the deck, I was able to see the flashing red and blue lights.

Two officers came into my bedroom. "We have R.L. apprehended. Is this where he lives?"

"Yes, that's my husband."

"We were called because there was a domestic disturbance. So, ma'am, were you involved?"

"Yes," I said.

"Ma'am, we're here to take your statement of what happened," said the officer.

"He was holding me down. I somehow managed to get up and run to the phone to call you."

"R.L. is on parole so we have to take him in. Do you have any drugs in the household?"

"No, we don't do that officer." The room was spinning. I felt light headed. I fell to the ground. The officer radioed for a paramedic. The fire department and paramedics came. The paramedic took my blood pressure.

"Your pressure is very low and you have a slight fever." They told me. I was dizzy and the room was spinning. "We need to admit you to see the hospital."

"No! I don't want to go," I said. "I have a kidney infection and I'm on antibiotics."

"When your husband fled, he had quite a bit of money on him," he said like he was suspicious about something.

"Yeah, he probably took it out of our safe."

"This is a pretty nice house," he said.

"Thanks," I said.

"What do you and your husband do for a living to afford a house like this? Since your husband was on parole, we have the right to search your home." This was the first time in my life ever dealing with police.

"Go ahead and search." I was too weak to think or argue. Four other officers came inside and started searching my home. I was so tired; I just wanted them out. When the fire department, medical emergency staff, and police finally left, it felt like the most surreal experience. What just happened? was all I could think. My home was ransacked and looked as if a tornado had run through it. Not once, before I dialed 911, did I consider the implications. R.L. had thirty days left on parole, and this was a violation. He was charged with a crime and they arrested him on the spot.

Two days later was R.L.'s arraignment. Like in the movies, I assumed that they would hold him for the night and release him the next morning. They didn't. The next day was the arraignment. R.L. came out in shackles and a green jump suite. I sat quietly and listened to the pending charges. I was listed as the victim. The court read out the charges. "Bail set at one million dollars," said the judge. The judge announced the next court date, which was to be next week.

The house was still a disaster zone. I hadn't cleaned. The kids were staying with family. I had been awake for 48 hours. Every thought brought a new worry. I had only enough money saved to last a few months on my income. Now that I was back to work we had just started to see a little light in our financial tunnel. We were barely holding on and had recently lost our rental property to foreclosure because we could no longer afford the payments. We were struggling each month trying to come up with the funds to pay the mortgage for the home we lived in.

I decided it was best to hire an attorney. I called J.B's dad, Mr. Barnes, and asked him if he knew a criminal attorney. He referred me to his friend Jeffery. At the appointment, I asked the attorney, "Can't I just tell the courts it was a mistake?"

"If they find out you were lying on the stand, you could also be charged with a crime."

"I wasn't hurt though," I said.

"The report says that the paramedics had to be called," the attorney shot back. "The District attorney takes on the case. You and your husband each need to retain different attorneys," the attorney advised. Both attorneys were charging thousands of dollars.

A week had passed, and I was back in court. There was a list of other cases that the judge had to work through before ours. Court cases are public hearings, so anyone can listen to the cases and testimony. The judge walked in and called the first case. A white guy in his 30's with shoulder length brown hair combed to the back stood next to an older white gentleman with silver hair who wore a red tie and white shirt with beige slacks. They stood at the courtroom podium.

There was a girl sitting on the other side of the podium, who I assumed was the guy's wife. They were a fit couple in their early thirties. The district attorney started to read the list of the guy's charges. "The defendant put a gun to the victim's head and yelled that he would pull the trigger. The victim at this time begged and pleaded for her life. The defendant than took the butt of the gun and hit the victim in the temple," stated the district attorney. The victim was his wife. She sat there silently as, the silver haired man defended his client.

"Is there a protection order filed?" the judge asked the district attorney. She was a middle-aged white woman who took her job very seriously, rightfully so.

"Yes, Your Honor. A protection order had been filed. Defendant will be under home custody. Bail set at $250,000." Seriously, why wasn't this guy going to jail? I asked myself.

The next day, I had to attend court ordered domestic abuse victim counseling at an agency called Next Door. I signed in and waited in the lobby to be called in for the appointment. Next to me sat a Mexican lady in her twenties with two small children. "I don't know what I'm going to do," she said out loud. I looked around to see if she was talking to someone else, but it was only the two of us and her children in the lobby area. "What's your story?" I asked her. She explained that her and her children's father got in a dispute after he came home drunk one night. It was late and the neighbor called the cops. Her man was put in jail and now being extradited back to Mexico. She didn't know how she and her children would survive on their own.

I was called into my session. The counselor handed me a photo copied paper that was titled, The Wheel of Violence. There was a circle in the middle of the page and in the center of this wheel it said, in bold, "Power and Control." Around the wheel were lists of things along with examples of domestic abuse. "We have a class on Tuesday," said the counselor. "You will attend that and then we will give you the document that you have to show the courts. Do you have any questions?"

"Do you have any housing assistance?"

"Yes, we have a women and children's shelter."

"What about assistance with paying the mortgage if your husband is locked up?"

"No, we just have the shelter. You can try the housing authority," she suggested

"What about financial assistance?"

"You can go to the Social Service Department and apply for assistance," then she handed me a flyer for the Welfare department.

Yes, R.L. and I argued; we even had a prior incident where things got physical. I wasn't sure if I could trust him, but he didn't try to control me. I had never felt powerless when I was with him. I had many mixed emotions. Could I be battered and not even realize it? When I got home, the doorbell rang and a guy handed me an envelope and told me that I had been served. I was being subpoenaed_ to court to testify against my husband. Part of the court document said that if I choose not to testify, I could receive jail time and/or a hefty fine. The reality of what I was living sunk in.

During the next bail hearing, the attorney was only able to get the bail reduced to $750,000 and that was still too much. I visited R.L. and took the baby as often as I could. R.L. called the house often. Sometimes, when he called, he was peaceful; other times, he was combative and angry.

I wished that I could bail R.L. out and have him back home so that we could start all over again, but that wasn't the reality. The situation was no longer in my hands. My love for R.L. was deep—deeper than anything I had ever felt for anyone besides my children. Was I wrong for this? I didn't see R.L. as an abuser. I saw him as someone, like myself, who was on an emotional roller coaster.

R.L. and I spoke on the phone that night. "They have me in the domestic violence program here. It's cool though—better than doing nothing," said R.L.

"I miss you and the kids have been asking about you," I said.

"You know, I could possibly get twenty-five years to life for this whole thing."

"They can't give you that much time!" I said.

"Because of what you said to them."

"I didn't want to lie, I just said—"

"Shush! We can't talk about the case over the phone. Also, were not supposed to be talking period," said R.L.

"I was still trying to work with the mortgage company on a loan modification to reduce our payments." Because real estate prices were dropping around the country, I owed way more on my house than it was worth. After R.L. was arrested, I could no longer afford the payments on my own, and I was now in default.

In the morning, I was in the kitchen making a cup of tea, when all of a sudden I heard a drilling sound. The sound was so loud that the sound vibrated threw out the house. The drilling noise was coming from my front door. 'Is someone breaking in?"I thought to myself. My heart was racing. With phone in hand, I was ready to call someone for help. The drilling stopped.

I looked out the window and saw a man dressed like a handyman, wearing jeans and a tool belt, clipboard under his arm with a drill in his hand walking up the driveway. He walked back towards the door and started drilling the door handle once again. I snatched open the door. "What the hell are you doing!" I yelled.

With a startled look on his face said,"Oh, this home is listed as vacant. It's in foreclosure, and I'm changing the locks," he said.

"Well it's not!" I said and slammed the door in his face. He walked down the long driveway to a white van.

The truth was, I hadn't been in touch with the mortgage company in months. When they called, I didn't answer. I applied for the modification and left it at that.

Life was unraveling. As the mound of bills, papers, and junk mail grew larger, so did the discomfort about where my life was headed.

Deep down inside, I felt neglectful, ashamed, and like my situation was out of control.

A couple of months after the drilling incident, I was in court once again, but this time standing at a podium in front of a judge, pleading with him not to foreclose on my home. I had prepared a full statement about how I was a single parent, I was dealing with a hardship, and that I had the possibility of reduced payments—along with a bunch of other compelling reasons why my home should be spared foreclosure.

The judge then said, "Although, your story is very compelling Mrs. Billops, the law is the law. Unless you have $35,560, we will have to proceed with the foreclosure ruling. I'll give you an additional thirty days to move." That was the ruling. I sat outside the courtroom waiting for the court reporter to complete my documents. An older African American lady with dreads sat down beside me on the wooden bench outside of the courtroom. She said, "Honey everything will be alright. I have a 2 bedroom in Los Gatos for rent." I was still in shock and denial. I wasn't going to leave my home. I thanked the lady and took down her information knowing I wasn't going to call.

At times, I felt as if I was watching my life on a movie screen, having no control over the outcome, or the ending. I just wanted the nightmare to be over. I stopped answering the phone for a few days. I wasn't sure if it were a debt collector, my husband calling from jail, or some other person calling to make me feel worse than I already did. I felt like a shell of the person I once was. My whole sense of reality was shaken. I was taught to work hard and reap the benefits. The harder I worked, the worse my life seemed to get. I couldn't take it anymore.

My life was spiraling out of control at a pace that I was struggling to keep up with. Bad things kept happening. I needed peace.

No matter how hard things were, I had to continue living for my children. Besides dreams of better days ahead, my kids gave me the fuel to keep going. These days, life was like a hazy fog. Once I considered taking my own life, something inside of me said, it's time to make a medical appointment. I was in the medical office the next morning. During the appointment, I sat in a room and the doctor asked me a series of questions. She asked me what brought me into the office. I told her about the problems that I was having, and how I considered ending my life. I was diagnosed with severe depression and anxiety. I was prescribed medication, individual counseling weekly, and group counseling twice a week.

Daily, I questioned myself; *how did I get here?* Just a few short years earlier, my life seemed to be going great. I was newly married, happy or I thought I was, and had a successful business. Why was I now going through so much turmoil in life? It used to be exciting, now life was just a struggle. I longed to find purpose, and the meaning out of all this. So, I began my search.

Reflection

"If you make a habit of buying things you do not need, you will soon be selling things you do." –Filipino Proverb

If it weren't for my daughter being born, I would have deemed 2007 - 2009 the worst years of my life. My whole foundation of reality was shaken. Right away, I learned to never take the things you love for granted. In just a few short months, everything was gone—my marriage, business, house, and other cherished relationships. Essentially, the foundation that I stood on was shaken violently.

My definition of depression is the void of happiness. Often times, depression can be all consuming and can lead to self-sabotaging behaviors. Anxiety can make us feel like we don't have control of our bodies, and depression can make us feel like there's no way out. Depression is very serious because it robs happiness from those who suffer with it, and most of all, it robs them of their true identities. I finally realized that me being depressed was cutting myself off from my dreams. Now that I am in a better place, I can look back and see that living was the best decision I made. I knew right away that something was wrong when I considered ending my own life. Unbeknownst to my friends and family, I was suffering. If you've ever thought about ending your life, the best decision you can make is to tell someone.

Chapter 12

Social Networking

*A*fter a few days of taking the meds the doctor prescribed me, I flushed them down the toilet. I wasn't a pill kind of person. When I used them, I felt numb and kind of like a zombie. I didn't want to be numb and not feel. I just didn't want to feel hopeless anymore. I wanted my life back.

After a couple of months in counseling, the feeling of hopelessness that I once had subsided a bit. It was time, more than the counseling, that helped, I think. While attending group counseling, I also came to realized that, at the end of the day, there are a lot more people in this world that have it tougher than I have it.

The day finally came when I had to move out of my home. There were many items that I couldn't take. I packed the most important things and sold some furniture, appliances, and other things I couldn't take to my new place. I packed boxes and put them onto the moving truck. Once everything was moved out of my house, I solemnly walked across the dirt scuffed cream tiled floors towards the glass sliding doors that lead to the outer deck that wrapped around the home. As I looked out onto the horizon, I thought to myself, *most of all, I will miss the view.* As I thought about having to leave my home, that intense, heavy feeling of sadness started to come over me.

It was time for me to move on. I remembered when Nana told me, "Whenever God takes something away, there's always something better to come."

I moved myself and my two children into a two-bedroom apartment across town. I so badly wanted to move somewhere far, far away, and make a new start somewhere else, but I couldn't decide where I wanted to move. Now that the house was gone, I wanted to leave everything behind and forget about everything that had happened. Deep down inside, I knew it would be best for the kids to stay near friends and family for support.

I imagined one day possibly moving to Los Angeles, Miami, or Las Vegas, to start a new life. I pondered the thought of getting back into modeling, but wasn't sure what that would be like as the mother of two children. Often, I thought about the state of my marriage and how everything was impacting my children. I wondered if I could have made a better choice. It wasn't hard for me to feel sorry for myself. It was easy to be the victim. I was tired of being down; I was ready to move on with life, but in reality, I told myself I couldn't move on, just forward.

The courts had issued an automatic protection order for me against R.L. Even though I told them I didn't fear for my life or want the protection order. They said it was standard law for domestic violence cases, and I would have to go back to court if I wanted to change it. So, I could no longer visit R.L. He was transferred to a California State Prison for his sentence. Even though the incident happened months prior, my mind kept wanting to reply the scenario in my mind between R.L and I that night. I dwelled on the part I played in the destruction of my marriage. How could I have reacted or acted differently that night? Was R.L. actually cheating on me? Was there any way I could have treated the situation differently? I also had many contradicting feelings about that night. I questioned R.L.'s loyalty and wondered how the scenario would have played out if I had never called the police. Would he have started to abuse me? Becoming more aggressive and violent over time with me? If I would have just let it go would I have eventually become a "true" victim of domestic violence? Even though, I missed R.L., him being taken out of our home so abruptly seemed like the death of someone close to me. I missed his smile, his smell. The kids missed him. He was in the process of being transferred to another prison and it had been weeks since I had spoken to him. I didn't know the state of my marriage. I was so lonely. The no contact order made it impossible to visit.

The doctor suggested that I go on medical stress leave from my tech job, and after being gone for more than a month, I was eventually replaced.

Now that I was ready to work again, I didn't have a job. I made a difficult decision to visit the social services office. When I arrived, I took a number and sat in the back of the lobby in the county building. I heard a familiar voice from behind, "Hey girl!" I knew that voice from somewhere. I slowly turned around and there she was, a girl I had known in middle school.

"Hey!" I said wanting to melt into the floor like an ice cream cone on hot cement. She was an old friend from middle school. Damn, I thought to myself.

"Girl, I work here. What are you doing here?" the middle school acquaintance asked in a nosey, but concerned voice.

"I'm here to get some documents signed," I said. That was the quickest excuse I could come up with without letting her know that I was really applying for welfare.

"Anyway girl, I'm here just to pick up my check. I work here." She repeated.

"Oh, okay," I said, even though I was thinking, yeah right and so do I.

When the kids were at daycare and school, when I wasn't searching for jobs, I had some spare time. So, I thought, why not take some up to date photos. I reached out to a photographer I had worked with in the past and started taking pictures again. Going on photo shoots started as nothing serious; I just wanted some updated digital images of myself. But, while doing so, I realized that this was a part of me that I had missed. I set up a social media account with a new alias. Being online made me forget about my problems. It was like a whole other cyber world away from the life that I was currently living. As I posted pictures on my social media page, I gained more followers. Online I friended people in the entertainment industry who I could possibly network with. People were making comments on my photos and asked to see more. I also got a lot of random guys sending direct messages trying to hook up. I enjoyed the attention, but wasn't interested. In addition, I also got legitimate requests for work. I started to feel alive again. For once in a long time, I started to forget about my problems.

A large casting agency in Los Angeles reached out to me via email about a reality show they were casting for, and asked if I would be interested in attending the audition. I submitted a few more photos and the casting director called to ask a few basic questions over the phone. Afterwards, she emailed over disclosures and a contact that I had to email back. The show was being shot for a huge network. If I was chosen, I would possibly have the opportunity to live in Los Angeles for a few weeks. The following weekend I headed down to LA to audition for the show.

I wondered if this would be my big break. The show was a dating show, and I was currently separated, not single. I was sure it was all acting and fake anyway. *Maybe me being married could be an entertaining twist.* I thought.

As soon as the camera started rolling, I drew a blank—just a blank stare into the camera. I wasn't chosen to move forward to the actual taping of the show. Not being chosen for the taping turned out to be a disappointing blessing in disguise.

One evening, when I was checking my messages on my social media account, one of the messages I received said, "I really like your pictures." I happened to check out the profile and it was a guy who, on his profile, claimed he played for the NFL. There were photos of an attractive black guy and it listed that he played for Oakland. I shook a thought of O.J. out of my mind. I thought the message and profile were probably a fake, but decided to respond anyway just for the fun of it. "Thanks for the compliment! May I see a pic of you?" I typed along with my personal email address.

A few minutes later, I received an email in my inbox. My heart started racing. It was a personal reply back to my request—a selfie that resembled of the guy in the social network photos. I emailed him a quick reply, "Nice! Thanks for the photo. Just wanted to make sure you were you…lol."

Eventually, we exchanged phone numbers and after talking on the phone a few times, he seemed like a cool person. I agreed to meet with him at a public place in a central location near a movie theater and restaurants. Before I got there, I started having second thoughts. It was about 7pm and the sun was starting to set, but it was still warm out. I saw him standing there waiting for me, and my heart was pounding. I started to get very nervous. It was really him, and I couldn't believe he wanted to meet me for a date! I would have expected him to have all kinds of girls waiting in line for him.

He wasn't very tall and a little thinner than I expected, but he was good looking and reminded me a lot of R.L. There was a Spanish restaurant in the plaza that we met at, so we decided to go there. I was so nervous that I didn't order anything, but a soft drink and guacamole dip. He ordered his food and a soft drink. We took a seat at a table near the bar. While we were there, one person did recognize that he played in the NFL.

While waiting for our drinks, we made small talk.

"So, tell me a little bit about yourself," I said. He told me that he was from Texas. We talked a lot about the difference between California and Texas.

"People are different," he said.

"What do you mean?" I asked

"Just the people that I work with act strange. Like they all think it's cool to mess with the same girls and everyone runs in a circle. A lot of the girls I date from here have boyfriends. You know what I mean? Is that a California thing?" he asked. I quickly changed the subject.

"What are you looking for?" I asked him

"I'm just looking for someone who's real."

"What about children?" I asked

"After I'm married, I eventually want kids," he said. In my head I thought, strike 2 for me. He didn't really ask me any personal questions, so I didn't let him know that I was separated from my husband or had children. He didn't ask. After dinner, he suggested that we walk over to the theater and see a movie. We saw a Comedy staring Will Ferrell.After the movie, he invited me to his apartment in a luxury community.

He had an alarm system. Inside the apartment was nicely decorated with expensive looking furniture. The first thing he did after going inside was get on his computer and check his email. While he checked his email, I looked around at the pictures on the fire place mantel. I checked around his house to see if there were items left behind from other women. I saw a picture of a dark-skinned, older couple on the fireplace mantel.

"Are these your parents?" I asked him.

"Yes!" He said. He told me to come to the computer desk he was sitting at so he could show me other pictures of his family. I could tell that he was close to his family and came from a nice Christian home; he had two parents and a sister. I didn't know many black people whose parents were still together.

We hugged and kissed each other goodbye. After I left, I knew I couldn't pursue a relationship with this man or pull him into my drama.

Through social media, I read that one of the top urban photographers that I followed would be in my area. I thought, *Fuck it…why not?* And over some recent images of myself. Later that day, I received a reply back from the photographer saying that he was interested in shooting with me.

The shoot was located in a hotel room near the San Francisco airport. When I arrived at the room, there were two girls already there. I overheard their conversation, and they were both cheerleaders for an NFL team. The room was a double suite with backdrops and lighting situated in each room. I put on my makeup in the bathroom while he finished up the shoot with the other girls.

"It's nice to finally meet you Sasha!"

"Thanks! Nice to finally meet you as well!" I said.

He was a little different from the rest of the photographers I had worked with in the past. He was young, athletic, and African American. We started our shoot. I nervously stood on the white back drop. 'You have a nice silhouette Sasha, and you're very pretty." He went on to say, "I thought you would have a bigger booty."

After he made that comment, my confidence subsided a little. I realized that I wasn't going to be anyone's idea of what they thought I should be. I was me. Not someone else's idea of me.

After months of not speaking to R.L., I finally received a call from him.

"My boy said he seen you out with some guy," He said.

"What are you talking about?" I asked. In my head I thought, damn news travels fast in prison, or he could be making this up and using reverse phycology.

"You were at the movies with some dude," he said. "Who is he?"

"You're going crazy," I said. "I've been at home taking care of the kids and trying to survive!" I shouted at him. When we hung up, I was upset. We only had fifteen minutes to talk, and we argued the whole time.

As I managed my modeling career on my own, the exposure led to other opportunities, like podcast radio interviews. I was featured in a few hip hop music videos for local artists, and in two magazines. I even had other models reach out to me for support and ask me questions about how to break into the industry. I had the star of the reality show, *Making the Band* reach out to me. Even with all of this attention, I didn't feel like I had broken into anything yet. Appearances were deceiving. I just had lost my home, my car was on the verge of repossession, and I was a single mother struggling just like the rest. Even so, I kept pushing forward and networked with some local models that reached out to me for advice. I was able to find them gigs for runway shows, local music videos, and promotions. As the models I referred worked these gigs, they built their portfolios for free in the process. I assisted other girls with scheduling photo shoots with local photographers for trade. I built a website to showcase the model portfolios. I did it because I enjoyed doing it. It built my confidence in the process and made me forget about my problems. When I was passionate about the things I did, I was good at them. Not because I was being paid to do it.

Porscha started working on her music career, and I was helping her find a beat for a new song she was writing. Porscha also asked me if I could manager her singing career while I was in between work. We were thinking about sampling a beat for a cover song on her demo. I came across various music artists while trying to suggest a song for Porscha to cover. On the social network, I scrolled down the lists of pages until one caught my eye. It was a picture of a rap artist I recognized. I liked his tattoos and thought his was cute. I decided to leave a comment on the picture.

I received a phone call one day from the district attorney's office. It had been nine months since R.L was arrested and the day before my birthday. "Am I speaking to Mrs. Billops?"

"Yes, this is her," I said.

"I'm calling to let you know there has been sentencing in the case and the defendant received six to eight years in prison," the lady on the other end said it to me like it was supposed to be good news, but not in my case. It was hard to accept what I was hearing. The reality was that R.L. could spend up to eight years of his life in prison.

After checking my inbox a few days later, I received a reply message from the rap artist who's picture I made a comment on. I was flattered that he actually responded back. He was a popular music artist; I heard his songs on the radio, and he had actually responded to my comment. I quickly responded back, "Feel free to call or text me." I left my phone number without really thinking much about it.

I was invited to a magazine release party in Los Angeles. The magazine was geared toward urban men which showcased glamour photography of female pin-up models from around the world. I received an email from the owner and editor of the magazine and he personally wanted me to be there. I replied to the email promptly letting him know that I would love to come to the party. I was so excited; I couldn't help but to smile as I replied back to the email.

I headed down to LA a couple weeks later. Porscha agreed to come along with me for support. I wore a black see-through lace lingerie dress with a cute black lace bra and panties underneath. I usually didn't dress this skimpy, but I felt I needed to make a lasting impression. We arrived early and sat in the VIP Section of the club. There were many other models that I recognized from online, various print ads, and music videos. I met the owner of the magazine—a dark-skinned black man who was in his late thirties or early forties. I introduced myself, "Hi I'm Sasha and this is my girl Porscha. I drove out from the Bay Area to be here," I said. I hoped that this opportunity would lead to more opportunities. We shook hands, and I looked him in his eyes and smiled. He thanked me for coming.

There were a lot of people at the party. Most of the night, I sat in the VIP section looking pretty with Porscha as security surrounded us. Men stood around and gawked at the models. When

I arrived back home from the party, I was a little annoyed. My appearance didn't lead to a feature in the magazine. I felt like it was a waste of time.

A photographer that I was working with submitted my photos to a different magazine, the liked the photos and decided to feature me in their magazine. This was the first magazine I was published in.

I went to test shoot for a TV show pilot, and a test shoot for Playboy. The same casting agency who sent me to the audition for the reality show contacted me again; this time, looking for extras to play a role in a new movie filming in San Francisco. It was a movie staring Rob Lowe. I wasn't sure what the movie was about, but thought it would sound good on my resume.

I enacted the scene of the pastor's wife, but had no speaking lines. I drove to San Francisco.When I got to the set, the extra's sat in a small dressing room in a historical church, where one of the scenes were being shot outside. The church was beautifully decorated with wood beams. We all waited eagerly to be called onto the set. One of the casting directors said that they were looking for an actress to play a night club role, and they thought that I would be perfect for it.

Finally, they called the extras. "Can I have you and you right here?" the director said pointing to me and a black gentleman. "Can I have you stand right here?

'Act as if you are greeting the congregation as they walk into the church." I stood next to Rob Lowe. I was so excited. Before that day, I didn't know who that was. After we were done, They kindly provided lunch for the extras.

I was contacted by the casting director later that evening and told me that after looking at the film, he realized that there were already too many shots of me next to the star actors and they couldn't offer me the scene.

Even though all of these opportunities were coming about, I wasn't making any money. I went from castings to photoshoots to magazine shoots, but wasn't getting paid for any of it. I filed documents for people and did other odd jobs just to get by. After I subtracted childcare and gas, I didn't even have enough to pay for groceries or rent. Modeling gigs paid very little to nothing, and most of my assignments and gigs were Time for Print or for exposure. For me, this modeling lifestyle was an illusion. I had ten dollars to my name and struggled to make ends meet.

One day, I received a text from a number in Atlanta. Since, I had lived in the south while I attended college, I recognized the area code. The text read, "What's up?"

I replied, "Who's this?"

The next text said, "DeAndre." I didn't know a DeAndre, so I called the number back. A guy answered the phone. "What's up," he said.

"Who's this?" I asked.

"DeAndre. You told me to call you!" Then, all of a sudden, a bell rang in my head. DeAndre was the hip hop artist that I had been messaging back and fourth on the social networking site.

"Oh hey what's up!" My heart started beating fast. "I can't believe you actually hit me back."I said.

"Yeah, most rappers have someone else managing their social networking sites, but I control my own shit," he said.

After that initial conversation, we started talking on the phone and exchanging text messages regularly. When we talked he held a conversation, but I could tell that he was kind of reluctant. He had mentioned a bad experiences with other female that he had met through social media. 'She tried to expose and black mail me." He said. Surprisingly, our conversations were actually very interesting and entertaining. When we talked, he asked me a lot of questions about myself. He asked if I had kids, was I married, where I lived, etc.

After I got off the phone with him on evening, I googled him to see what I could dig up. It's wasn't hard to find gossip about him. One of the blogs said that he had a girlfriend. It's not like I cared too much since I was in a relationship myself. I just thought we were being truthful with one another. The next time I talked to him, i asked him about it.

'That relationship is for publicity." He *said*, insinuating that someone behind the scenes set them up to boost his record sales.

I shared with him various pictures that I took during photoshoots. Finally, at one point he felt comfortable enough to send me some pictures. When we talked on the phone, I told him that I was going back to school to become a teacher. I decided that since the real estate market was so unstable, I decided that I would go back to school. When we got on the subject of school, DeAndre told me about his school experience and living in with his father in Mississippi. Saying that he decided to leave school because he had a number 1 hit on the radio and because of this the teachers where trying to sleep with him.

He told stories about celebrities he had met, and the ins and outs of the music industry. He was adamant that he started a movement in hip hop that he wasn't recognized for. 'New artists in the industry stole my style."he said.

He disclosed how other rappers in the industry sometimes hired body doubles to perform shows and greet fans. "A lot of artists have body doubles," he said. I was shocked, and it didn't sound like he was lying.

"How would your students feel about you modeling?" DeAndre asked.

"They wouldn't know," I said.

"If you promoted yourself correctly, how wouldn't they know?" He shot back. I quickly imagined how a scenario could play out if my students saw the racy photos that I was taking. I now saw it from a new perspective. That conversation was a turning point for me. I couldn't straddle the bridge any longer. I had to choose what was more important. Modeling was getting in the way of the things that I really wanted.

Most of the time DeAndre spoke rationally, but some times he acted just plain strange.

I started a new part-time substitute teaching job at a middle school near my home. While I was at work, DeAndre called. I called him back during my lunch hour.

"I'm ready to get married!"

"Okay, to whom?"

"You!"

"I'm already legally married, and besides, we've never even met in person."

"You're a good person, and I think I can trust you."

"Sure," I said.

"Can you do me a favor?" he asked. "Like, I really need you to do this for me."

"Okay, what is it?" I asked.

"I need for you to go pay my phone bill, and I'll put the money back into your account in a few days."

"What?" I asked, confused that he would even have the audacity to ask me to pay his bill, but I did. I paid the bill over the phone with my credit card with him on three-way.

"You would probably be too boring for me," he said. 'But I still wanted to meet up." He had a concert coming up in the Bay Area. We made plans to meet up afterwards.

The next evening, I called him and some female picked up.

"Hello," she said.

"Umm, can I speak to DeAndre?" I asked.

"Who the fuck is this?" she asked. I then heard a scuffle and the phone went silent. I tried calling him back, but he didn't answer and didn't return my call that evening. I felt like I may be getting played, so I decided to cancel the payment that I made for his phone bill the next morning.

The next day my phone rang and the call was from DeAndre. I was kind of afraid to answer the phone, but I did. He was pretty upset that I cancelled the payment.

A small sum of unexpected money came in. I had to use this money so that I could get back on my feet. My goal was to use the money as leverage and invest it in another business. I couldn't find a job that provided enough, and I needed to make something happen. This seemed like the only decision I had at the time. I had expertise in all kinds of things. I did some research and came across a solicitation, work-from-home opportunity. It was a company who sold credit card processing terminals and software.

They sent me the application and contract. I received it, signed it and faxed it back. This was my ticket to success! That's what I told myself. I couldn't wait to get started on my new business venture. I would get paid ten days after a customer signed up or purchased a credit card terminal. I had a lot of experience in sales and knew that I could lead a direct sales team.

It was morning and I went to the deli to grab bagel. A black man in his thirties came up to me, "Hello, my business is hiring sales staff." He handed me a card. I told him that coincidentally I was a real estate agent and business owner looking for sales staff of my own to hire. 'Is that right, I may have a small office space for lease if your interested. He said. I thought everything was falling into place. I was looking for an office space. I called the guy the next day and met him at the office he had for rent. It was small, but I could make due. He invited me to lunch the next day to discuss the details of the sublease. It was the next day and the guy pulled in a red Maserati. During lunch he started talking about modeling and how he was throwing a fashion show. I wasn't there to talk about modeling so I quickly changed the subject. Once we agreed to the terms of the sublease, I met him later that night with the deposit.

The next day the guy was suppose to meet me at the office with the keys, but he didn't show up. Before calling the guy, I knocked on office door, but no one answered.

He never answered when I called, but called back later that day. He said that he had an emergency to tend to and that his business partner had the key on him and was out of town. He suggested that I could conduct the sales applicant interviews at his other office in the mean time. Due to my desperation, I agreed and called everyone that I had scheduled an interview with and told them the new address.

The next morning, I arrived fifteen minutes early at the other office. It was a small office building that had individual suites. I knocked on the office suite. The guy opened to door. I peered in. It looked like he slept there. There was a futon mattress on the floor and it smelled of body order and cheap cologne.

I quickly helped him straighten up. There was one desk and a chair. I left the door open to air out the office. Six applicants showed up and I conducted the interviews to hire sales agents for my new business.

After conducting the interviews, I decided to go to the property manager to see what the deal was with the office I had paid for. Something didn't seem right with this guy. The property manager disclosed to me that the guy hadn't paid rent and was behind a couple months. He actually owed three times the amount that I paid him, so the landlord changed the locks. The property manager felt bad that I got taken and said that he would consider renting the suite to me. I filled out the application and we scheduled a meeting for the next morning. In the meantime, I called the guy to get my money back. No answer.

It was the next morning, and I came back to the office for the meeting with the property manager. He said, "I considered actually renting to you until I Googled your name and saw this." He showed me ALL of the pictures I had posted. I had never Googled my name so I didn't know what came up. "I know you're running a prostitution ring," he said.

"What?!" I gasped. "That's ridiculous!" I would have started laughing if I weren't so insulted. "That's not true," I said. The lump in my throat was so big that no words came out. Then, I was finally able to mutter. "That is not true!" My eyes started to water, and I got up without saying a word and walked out of the office. I had never been so insulted and so disgusted. I drove to the guy's office where I had conducted the interviews. He was there.

"Give me my money back!" I said.

"I don't have your money."

"I gave you hundreds of dollars," I said. "You're a con artist and a crook."

"Take me to court!" he said and closed the office door.

I drove back home and typed him the nastiest email ever and sent it to the guy. Then, I got onto Craigslist and began looking for office suites. I already had my mind set on starting the business and had convinced myself that I needed an office to conduct the business. Everything that was going on was just merely a minor setback. I was going to make this business successful no matter what. I remembered hearing about entrepreneurs who had taken their last and invested it into a business and succeeding. How was I any different?

I found another office where I received the first month free. I had only thirty days to make some money. I quickly, hired a staff of people—including a receptionist, office manager, and a few tele-marketers. Everyone that I hired agreed to being paid thirty days after starting. One guy I hired was a highly paid office manager and worked for his company for many year. He was making about ninety thousand dollars a year at his current job, but he wasn't happy and wanted a change. I offered him a job as an office manager at my of-fice. The next day, he called me and said he quit his current job and would start the next day. I wanted to bring back the feeling that I had when I was at Tony's office for the first time.

I was doing all these things, but feeling like I wasn't getting any-where. The more I tried the more I lost. I couldn't afford to pay rent this month. The next day, I went into the apartment manager's of-fice. I told them that I could only take care of half the rent. "The best we can do is give you a week," said the manager. I heard that before. I knew I wouldn't have the money.

If I gathered up what little I had left to pay rent, I would have had $10.00 left in my purse to last me until the end of the month. There was a late notice taped to my door. On the top of the page it said, "3 Day Pay or Quit." I packed the few things that I had, which were mostly clothes, painting supplies, the kid's toys, and things I used day-to-day. We moved into the office suite. I had two young children depending on me. My only choice at the time was to move our things into the office for a few days until I figured things out. I would have to stay at the office with my children until I closed those deals and could afford a new apartment. Why were all these hardships and bad things happening? I just felt and knew I had to change something. I started to notice a pattern in my life.

I was convinced that I would find another apartment closer to the office in a few days. I told the kids that it was just temporary. I made it seem like an adventure. We had our sleeping bags and snacks. I didn't tell my mom or anyone else that I was evicted. If I did, I knew mom would over react and tell the whole family and the situation would be blown way out of proportion. It was hard, but I kept it to myself.

Some days, the stress seemed unbearable. I hid my feelings from the children. Although I was going through problems, I wanted to find the best way to raise my children without letting my problems affect them. I felt guilty that I couldn't give them the things that they deserved, but they were always my first priority.

One week living in the office turned into two weeks in the office. I started to feel drained. My office was my room. The restrooms in the office had two stalls with toilets and the third stall was a shower. The office "break room" was a small kitchen with a microwave, sink, and area for a fridge. During the day, the kids were at school and daycare.

At night, the kids were snuggled together fast asleep. My cell phone started ringing and illuminated the office, jolting me out of my sleep.

I sent the call to voicemail and attempted the fall back asleep until consciousness crept in. I was up for good. My thoughts started to race and wouldn't stop. I remembered that I had a joint hidden away in makeup bag, for times like this.

I filled up a large Rubbermaid plastic container with warm water to take a bath. The water felt so relaxing. I hadn't soaked in the bath tub in weeks. I imagined being in a warm bubble bath in my own home like old times. I snapped out of my day dream and reality sunk in. I was living out of an office suite with my children. I stepped out of the Rubbermaid container and looked in the mirror at my reflection and closed my eyes. I let the tears roll down my face. *How did I get here?* I asked myself.

My staff was doing a great job. After two weeks, we had several businesses that wanted to purchase credit card terminals. I realized I was in trouble with my business when the company we were distributing the terminals for had yet to pay us on any of the customers we sent over, and there was only 7 days left until pay day and rent due. I called into the distribution company and they started giving me excuses. The process was taking much longer than they promised. Eventually, after bugging them every hour for day, the credit card terminal company stopped responding to my emails and phone calls. I was in a major dilemma; I didn't even have enough to pay my overhead and staff. I prayed that everything would come through. Ultimately, I had to walk away from yet another business.

I called mom crying on the phone. I had two small children that I could barely provide for. I couldn't figure out how I would pay my bills once again. Mom asked me if we wanted to move in with her while I got back on my feet. At the time, I needed the stability. I also needed to focus my mind on something other than feeling sorry for myself. So, I found myself back at home with my mother. Lately, I had been mad at everyone: my family, friends, R.L, the court system. After losing yet another business, I was frustrated and confused. I needed to know what was happening to me and why I was seeing these "bad luck" cycles in my life.

One evening, Tonia called and I decided to answer. I thought maybe I needed to talk to my friends. If I did, maybe I would feel better. As soon as I said 'hello', instead of kindness, I heard an angry voice on the other end. "Why haven't you retuned any of my calls?" Tonia demanded. "You are so selfish for not answering." I didn't really say anything back, I just listened to her vent.

I pulled away from anyone who I honestly felt didn't have my back or best interest at heart. There were connections with friends that I questioned. One friend confessed to me that, when I was doing better than her, she was jealous. Even though I appreciated the heart to heart, I wasn't planning to be broke forever. The conversation made me rethink our friendship. I knew it would be hard to progress in life with a crowd full of people who called themselves friends, who deep down inside wanted to see my demise.

You are who you surround yourself with; so I started to evaluate the people who I spent the most time with. There was an emotional aspect to friendship and having to put so much effort into my friendships was emotionally draining. I felt the need to withdraw from everyone. I turned into an introvert and distanced myself. I had to get real with myself and develop my own way of thinking and not be influenced to think anything that wasn't aligned with who I was.

I wanted to find the deeper meaning of life. For months a friend that I met through real estate suggested that I watch the movie, The Secret. I put it off and hadn't had time until recently. The central theme of the movie was that, thoughts become things and the things that the thoughts become is the reality and experiences that we live day-to-day. The movie presented facts based on science and the overall theme was, if you change your thoughts, you can change your life and the experiences you live. After watching the movie, I thought about some of my life experiences and how they coincided with how I was thinking at the time. I realized that, when I've been in a negative feeling place, bad things happened.

I started to reflect on what I was thinking about in the most present moment. Lately, I had been emotionally up and down. When something good happened, I was happy; when something good wasn't happening, I was depressed. My emotions were becoming conditional to my surroundings and lately my surrounding weren't pleasing.

After doing a little research, I learned that many new age thinkers and philosopher's suggested meditation to quiet the mind. I decided to try meditation out. At first, it felt weird sitting quietly, trying to not think of anything. The first few times, I couldn't help but to think about things. What was it that I wanted out of life? I knew what I didn't want and usually focused on that, but according to what I was reading, I was doing my thinking backwards; I was supposed to focus on what it was that I wanted and not what I didn't want to happen.

I knew that I needed to look at life from a different perspective. I started to realized how much energy and effort anger and negative thinking took away from my children and doing other productive things. My conscience said, "Move forward, forgive, and give back."

I became almost obsessed with figuring out life and finding the answers to happiness. I researched String Theory. I also stopped going on social networks and chatting with people. I spent my time reading and researching. I started studying different religions. I learned to listen more from my heart and intuition. I learned to look at my life from a non-judgmental stand point.

I began to exercise every morning and took it easy when possible. I couldn't afford a gym membership so I stretched, walked, and jogged in the morning while imagining a new me. I just started doing things like staying in the warm shower, letting the water hit my hair and imagining that I were under a waterfall on a tropical island lying in the sun. Exercise was my outlet. As I ran, I imagined a happier life. I forced myself to exercise, then sat at the computer researching.

One night in 2011, I had a strange dream. In this dream, Grandpa Billy came to visit me. He was still suffering from Alzheimer's and wasn't doing too well, but in my dream he was healthy. In the dream he said that everything would be okay. He also reminded me of the conversation we had years ago when I was a child, and he told me that he wouldn't be around forever. He went on to say that him passing away was just a part of life and that he forgave me about the money years ago and that it was okay to move forward.

The next morning, I woke up and started to write down a few pleasant memories I had of Grandpa Billy, not knowing that what I wrote down would be the words I read to the audience during his funeral service.

I started teaching again. Professors motivated me when I wanted to quit. I went back to school and passed all the tests required to become a grade school teacher in California. I enjoyed working with children and eventually, being an educator overcame my desire to model. Working with children gave me a new perspective on life.

Reflection

Learning to have a more positive outlook took me some time, especially when my life wasn't going the way I thought it should. With practice, I learned to think more positively and become solution oriented.

For me, social networking had its disadvantages as well as advantages. If it is not used wisely, social networks can be a disadvantage. Social networks leave easy accessibility to invite others into our lives.

I had to lose almost everything to gain sanity. When I lost my material assets, I started to see a new reality. I realized that I wanted to be more of a role model and mentor, than live a Hollywood lifestyle. Modeling wasn't fulfilling my purpose; maybe it was just a stepping stone. It taught me how to handle rejection and maintain confidence.

A determined person who has the ambition to succeed wants to appear as if they have it all together. If they didn't appear to have it together, others may see them as weak. Trying to appease others before ourselves can take a toll on us. Should I have said something different? Why doesn't this person like me? Am I good enough? Being worried about how others perceive us causes tremendous stress. Stress causes anxiety and depression, and in turn starts to affect our mood and even our physical bodies.

Chapter 13

Discovering Success

"I have not failed 10,000 times—I've successfully found 10,000 ways that will not work,"
THOMAS EDISON.

I call September 28th, 2011 my rebirth day. On this day, I officially decided enough was enough. I was going to take responsibility for where I was in life and work from that day forward to get where I wanted to go. Too many times have I felt like I was over-qualified for a job—too intelligent just to give up. I was educated, intelligent, and experienced. Why did i keep failing? The biggest realization that I came to was that I was being someone else's idea of who I should be. When you only see yourself the way someone else has perceived you, you may very well possess a far-greater potential than you know. I knew that I could be my own worst enemy or best friend. Regardless of my gender, shape, size or complexion, I had to learn to love myself and until I did that, I wouldn't find true success or happiness.

I had to get to know myself before I knew what I believed. Only after finding out who I was and what I wanted to accomplish in life, was I able to establish the values that I wanted to utilize to attain the goal of success. Upon reflecting, I examined some virtues such as integrity, honesty, responsibility, etc., to evaluate how

I could utilize these virtues to get me to where I wanted to go in life. Having integrity supported me in transforming my life. When you have integrity in your actions, you will experience a state of completion with yourself and life. Having integrity is valuing yourself. This sets the stage on how others will treat you and feel when they are in your presence.

Being conscience is the key to success. Once something is learned, it's very hard to forget it. Keep in mind that change doesn't happen overnight, but if you implement consistency, change is bound to happen.

Here are 10 gradual changes that I made, which brought happiness and contentment into my life. Again, changing negative thinking patterns and the way I thought was a gradual process.

Step 1: Open your Mind to Various Possibilities.

When I opened my mind to various possibilities, I was opening myself up to a new world of options. The first step to opening my mind was exploring who I am and what makes me a unique person. I did this by separating myself, mentally and emotionally, from those who tried to identify who I was for me. I separated myself from the people that I felt may have limited me or held me back when I saw an opportunity to advance myself. People who limit your potential may be a person who has controlled your thoughts, or someone who has pushed you into acting out a role that is not becoming of you. I started realizing that I control my own destiny. I worked to let go of pain and started forgiving those who had hurt me. We also have to find forgiveness in our hearts for people who we think did us wrong. We don't have to call someone out or make them pay for their actions. When we confront someone for something they did to us and don't get the response that we wanted, it makes us feel worse and can make the situation worse. It's not our job to punish someone because they wronged us. It is a waste of time and energy. Life causes people to realize their actions towards others when the time is right. Once I forgive, pain had less control over my thoughts.

Step 2: Clear your Mind.

I started to practice meditation. At first, meditation for me was more or less a type of escapism. I would focus on my physical desires and envision peaceful scenes that many times made me smile. I would sometimes imagine sitting on a beach with white sand and could actually feel the warmth of the sun touching my skin. The times I became stressed, upset, or disappointed instead of focusing on the issue, I sat in a quiet place and envisioned I were somewhere else. The *Love, Light, Peace* mantra was tremendously helpful for me when I felt anxious or stressed. I took long, deep breaths and imagined being on a vacation. Quickly, I was able to reach the goal of achieving a tranquil state of mind; however, I realized it wasn't helping me to address my true life issues—birthing the desire to write about my life.

Step 3: Evaluate Your Experiences.

"The unexamined life is not worth living," said the ancient Athenians.

Going back and evaluating my history helped me better understand myself. Contentment is found in spiritual growth and personal growth. After I evaluated my life experience, I now had a basis for where many of my beliefs, thoughts, and even fears came from. I started to notice many coincidences and patterns in my life. I started to pay attention to the little synchronicities of life. This helped me realize my true desires.

Step 4: Be Aware of Your Thoughts.

Only through controlling my thoughts, was I able to control my happiness. I was diagnosed with major clinical depression. Everyone's brain works differently, but I became conscious that my mind had a predisposition to feeling down. Humans are emotional creatures. Many of our thoughts come from emotions. It was important for me to love myself, so that I could show others love regardless of how they treated me. I had to think differently to overcome challenges. I knew I needed to change the way I thought about things in my life in order to grow. The problem was, I didn't know where to start.

When I actually took time out to listen to my thoughts, I realized that they tended to jump around randomly, often landing on critiques, harsh judgments, and self-centered whining.

Changing the way we have been thinking and behaving for the last ten, fifteen, twenty years, or even our entire lives, can be tough. In our minds, we many want to change the way we think and approach things, but our physical response forces us into the same patterns day in and day out, year in year out. The hardest part about making changes to your life is having the will power to actually follow through with the change and gain the momentum to sustain lasting change.

Day to day, I started to notice how I was feeling, by being aware of my thoughts. When I did pay attention, I was able to change the focus and start thinking about more positive things. For example, when I started to think of other peoples' negative opinions of me, I would feel bad. So, instead I thought about spending a good time with my children or other things I enjoyed.

If you didn't have someone to tell you that you're worthy and capable of great things, it's okay, as long as you eventually realize it yourself. Realizing and knowing your self-worth is like unlocking the key to your heart.

Step 5: Define the Things That You Want.

I was turning 30 and no longer wanted to go through life just coping. My goal was to achieve life transformation and realize life for what it really was. I knew I wasn't put on the earth to be miserable and unhappy, or to live a mediocre existence. My goal was to find inner peace and happiness, thus removing dramatic disruptive episodes from my life completely. This is when I started to realize that life is a gift. That day, I started to take some quiet time for myself each day in search of what it was I truly wanted from life and what truly made me happy.

Step 6: Maintain Balance in Your Life.

We've all heard at some point that sometimes even the things we choose to eat have effects on mood, inhibitions, and emotions. Some of us are more sensitive to our environments than others. Some environments can even trigger negative memories. There are also people that have environmental allergies to alcohol, illegal drugs, or prescription drugs—all of which affect the mind. Too much sugar or salt, caffeine, red dyes, and high fructose corn syrup affect us all in different ways. Some people have an addictive personality and have a dependency on certain elements like alcohol, illegal or prescription drugs, relationships, etc. The clearest indication of dependency is when one uses something in excess to cope with stressful circumstances.

Many suffer from caffeine sensitivity and don't even know it, while others consume several cups of coffee throughout the day just to stay up and alert. That same coffee that keeps us functioning can have a negative impact on emotions, thoughts, and behaviors.

Drinking too much tea or chowing down on a bar of dark chocolate—both of which can contain nearly as much caffeine as a cup of coffee—can actually make stress worse.

Step 7: Desire to Eliminate BS

I had to stopping feeling sorry for myself. It took time to stop caring so much about what others thought about me or the choices that I made. I had to own up to my mistakes and move on. At times, I had to be hard on myself. I couldn't bring the BS from the prior year, month, week, or day into the present. I had to start thinking positively about myself. I began imagining a future that was different from my past; a future where things actually got better with each day. I stopped partaking in gossip on the phone and eliminated my day time TV watching. Now that I was focused on making my life better, I didn't have time for the BS.

Dwelling in misery will only make you feel worse for longer. I started to evaluate my surroundings. Some people have a way of bringing us down. Stress can be contagious. You can experience stress when someone you know is affected by a traumatic event, like a car accident or chronic illness.

Not every connection is meant to last forever. When you let go of something or someone, if it's meant for you it'll come back. Some connections are meant for learning. I know, walking away from a friendship may be one of those things that are easier said than done. But, when it's done you will feel so much better. If you're one of those people who truly values friendship, send a little prayer out to the universe to send true friends your way that will have your back and best interest at heart. Even if it's for the best, change can be difficult. The good thing is, once you have your mind made up, you can make it a gradual process. Although, many friendships of mine ran their course, I learned and grew from them.

Life didn't get better overnight. Just like anything else that's worth achieving, it took work and consistency. I attempted to reflect back and learn from my so called "bad" experiences or mistakes without associating guilt, regrets, or embarrassment about my actions. During my reflection, I realized that many people would have various opinions about my life or the decisions that I made. Many times, others meant well, but I had to trust my own instincts. Having high self-regard is very important to becoming successful. I learned a valuable lesson; I could never again make decisions based on fear, doubt, worry, or anger. Any decision made from a negative place would continue to grant me the negative consequences.

Step 8: Find What Motivates You.
Every person's realization of success is different. Most of us have an idea of what success means to us individually. Finding lasting happiness comes down to passionately reaching for the things you want and going after them with conviction. Don't do what others expect from you. Do the most that you are capable of. If you can dream it, you can achieve it. Use my life as an example for knowing that anything is possible if you really want it. Become your own definition of happiness and success.

I determined just what it was that I wanted to accomplish in life. I practiced being conscious in my decision making. I learned to focus on things that made me happy, regardless of the conditions in my life, society, or the world.

My motivators for starting a business had always been convenience and income. In the past, I never really considered the level of satisfaction I would get from the business, so when times got hard, I quit. Find something you are truly passionate about and make a great living doing it. Work with the skills, traits, and assets that you have. Anyone can have the life they want.

Many researchers suggest that people in prostitution, in general, suffer from "negative identities or lack of self-esteem. Although, Webster's Dictionary states the definition of prostitution is 'the act or practice of indulging in promiscuous sexual relationships in exchange for money', for the sake of my argument, I will stick with the general definition. Many of us are living a life that make us feel worse about ourselves, not better. Many of us have traded our dreams for a job, career, or lifestyle that's not fitting to our true ambitions. Life is about reaching our true potential. There are many people out there that are prostitutes and don't even realize it. Many of us use our time, talents, and abilities to do jobs that we hate for the sake of "earning money." The definition of a prostitute is 'a man or woman who willingly uses his or her talent or ability in a base and unworthy way, usually for money'.

Step 9: Always Strive for Better.

In time, I learned that when you truly love yourself, you will not accept certain things.

At least one time in your life, you have probably felt marginalized and stereotyped based on another's perceptions. To judge others is to judge oneself. When others are judging the exterior instead of the interior, they miss out on the true beauty of life. Some are obsessed with analyzing others. But, what we really need to do is analyze ourselves.

Anyone who is not fulfilling their true purpose in life is selling themselves short. Make a decision to live a purposeful life and stick with it. Life can be happy and meaningful.

It's never too late. We are all responsible for our own lives and decisions. My belief is that we sometimes have the urge to blame others for our unhappiness or for the choices we should or should not have made. By making someone else responsible, you are just shifting blame from oneself to another and still carry the negative feelings regardless. When someone tells us to move on, we easily make excuses for why me must stay. I am baffled by how many of us stay in miserable situations, while refusing to make the needed changes in our lives to find true happiness.

I didn't have very long to feel sorry about myself. At the end of the day, good or bad, I had to live with my decisions. I had children to take care of and a life to live. I didn't have a choice but to succeed. I learned to find forgiveness in my heart for past grievances. In order to move forward, this was a must. I realized that, in fact, I was creating these patterns in my life.

These days, if you are truly unhappy with a physical feature, you can change it. If you are unhappy with your weight, exercise! Changing the way you think about yourself is another thing. Only changing things on the outside doesn't change the way you feel within. No matter what you do or whatever mask you hide behind, you will always be you. We stand in the mirror at times and say, "I wish this" or

"I should do that." The reality is that it's not just about what we consider our physical "flaws". There may be things that we wish were done differently. There are times that I know I could have tried or done better. The reality is, the past is the past. The only thing that we can control is now. We have to change our ways now to have a better future.

At times, we need to be a little self-conscience to bring about positive change. Being self-conscience isn't the same as having low self-esteem. Many mix up the two. We all have an ideal self; it is knowing who you are capable of being. It's okay to know your faults, but don't acknowledge them often and never complain to others about them. Many people are jealous in nature. When there are those around you who perceive you are doing better than they are, they may one day use your fears and weaknesses against you.

I was one of those people who only felt good about themselves when others said pleasant things to or about me, or held me in high regard. In order to be successful, we have to have high self-regard regardless of what others think. That's why it is called, "self-esteem." Self-esteem is about self-awareness. If we do not believe in ourselves, how do we expect others to believe in us? Insecurity is when we start doubting our qualities. Most importantly, if others do not notice the good things we bring to the table, it just means we need to realize them in ourselves. Once we do, it will radiate outward. Life is like a mirror. If you perceive yourself in a low regard, others will perceive you in the same way that you see yourself.

Prostitutes give their value away for a price, and at the end, the prostitute loses integrity which is of the highest value of all. Prostitution is not, in fact, about selling sex, but selling your true value. Today, many of us are trading precious time and energy for money. Find your true purpose and happiness. If not, hate, drama, stress, anxiety, and depression proceed. These are not conditions that we have to live with.

Sometimes, we are not living the life that we desire, or do not have the finances we would like. Many of us have had conflict in our lives—negative events that happen to us. We may learn great lessons from such experiences, but certainly never want to relive them. If we do keep reliving them, it's usually because we are not allowing ourselves to learn the lesson. These experiences teach us what to do and what not to do in the future to avoid pain. Sometimes we can become too cautious if presented with a similar set of circumstances. Be cautious not to develop post-traumatic fears and use fear as an excuse.

Step 10: Be Determined.

Be determined to live a better life. When I stayed consistent and didn't give up, things started to change around me. You can start by not focusing so much on the things that cannot be changed or controlled. A good first step is to try not to think about the problems. This can be difficult if bill collectors are ringing your phone off the hook. But, couldn't you stop answering or change your number? I realized that my mind and thoughts create my perceived reality. Focusing on what isn't working only made my situation worse. Focusing on solutions improved my situation. Sometimes life takes us in a direction that we don't want to go, but there is a silver lining in every situation. Know that good can come from every circumstance.

I stopped expecting things to happen right away. I learned to be okay with time. Being patient was the key to my stability. I also stopped feeling sorry for myself and realized that life is really what I decided to make of it. I had to work to change the inside (how I thought) and if I changed that, the outer had to follow. I realized that the trials and tribulations were all worth it. My experiences taught me more than any pricy education. Experience was definitely my best teacher, and it helped me fine tune my desires. I realized that life works in perfect timing.

Reflection

> *The various features and aspects of human life, such as longevity, good health, success, happiness, and so forth, which we consider desirable, are all dependent on kindness and a good heart.*
> —Dalai Lama, Kindness Quote

Learning true life values with any experience is the key to feeling contentment. The concepts I learned, I considered important and invaluable because those are the experiences that cannot be replaced with money. The value is the true nature of who I am. Now that I know myself, I know what my life legacy is going to be. Now, I can focus my energy in a positive direction heading towards my dreams. Now, I can convey to others that side of me.

Note from the Author

Writing is a creative art form. Before I started writing, I've always done a bit of creating. For example, I've created good situations for myself, as well as some bad ones. I'm not going to lie. I've created some very bad situations. Yes, the truth can hurt. But, honesty can heal old wounds. And that's what I've decided to do—be brutally honest with myself and with you, of course. Thank you for giving me this outlet of self-reflection and expression. The greatest thing is having someone to listen to your story. I told you about where I come from and where I've been, and hopefully you too will learn something from my story—or at least entertained. My greatest hope is that, by you learning my journey, you will be inspired to try things differently.

Where was I? Oh yes, I've created meals out of Ramen noodles and left over chicken, I've created friends out of enemies, businesses, children, and money out of thin air. The hardest thing that I created for myself was success. That's because success can't be purchased, earned, or given. Success to me means happiness. It's a feeling of contentment, gratitude, and fulfillment. You are successful when you are serving your purpose. In order to find success, you have to work hard and pay attention to the things that matter.

About the Author

Tanisha has a Bachelor's of Art degree in Human Development and is currently an educator, certified to teach multiple subjects. She works with low income and inner city children and youth. Tanisha sees writing as an art form and as a vehicle to communicate with people around the world. Tanisha considers herself an artist and enjoys anything related to art. In her free time, she paints, writes, listens to music, and enjoys spending time with her husband and children.

Growing up in the 1980's and 90's in the world's leading hub for high-tech innovation and development wasn't easy. She grew up in the Silicon Valley during its most rapid time of growth and expansion. Her whole life has been a crazy adventure. Her experiences have given her an exceptionally interesting perspective on life.

Tanisha's 2016 release, The Prostitutes Guide to Success, earned her international recognition and numerous Up and Coming Author Awards.

Coming Soon...

Tanisha's future projects include the novel, *Lovely Lolita*—a sexy thriller with many twists and turns. It's a story about a young bi-racial woman who learns of a secret past that her mother has hidden from her. She decides to move to the west coast to pursue her dreams of being a professional dancer.

Behind the Wall is a biographical memoir; a true story about Tanisha and her husband, Robert, while they coped with the 2009 domestic violence charge that led to a conviction and an almost eight-year prison sentence. This novel is co-authored by both Tanisha and Robert Billops as they address the events that led up to that night and the years after.. They discuss how changing their outlook on life led to positive changes in their marriage and lives. They discuss the judicial system, the California prison system, and the processes designed to make black families fail. Discover how this young couple learned difficult life lessons, and realized the importance of being accountable for one's actions.

.

www.ingramcontent.com/pod-product-compliance
Lightning Source LLC
Chambersburg PA
CBHW062207270326
41930CB00009B/1675